THE *Fender* TELECASTER

THE DETAILED STORY OF AMERICA'S SENIOR SOLID BODY ELECTRIC GUITAR

BY A.R. DUCHOSSOIR

SPECIAL FOREWORD BY
JAMES BURTON & ALBERT LEE

HL® Hal Leonard Publishing Corporation

7777 West Bluemound Road P.O. Box 13819 Milwaukee, WI 53213

ISBN 0-7935-0860-6
First U.S. Printing October, 1991

CONTENTS

FOREWORD

Over the last few years, the idea of a Telecaster book has been frequently put forward to me, by collectors like Jeff Gray, Alan Rogan or Jim Werner as well as by my publisher. I guess it was probably a logical step to consider a companion to the Stratocaster book.

I took the plunge and now I hope this newest offering will live up to the expectations of the many people who assisted me one way or the other in its making. The list of acknowledgements is quite long indeed! But I specially wish to thank a few key individuals for their continuous support throughout this project, namely Jim COLCLASURE, John PAGE, Dan SMITH, John SPRUNG and my lady Sue.

I am also most appreciative of the written forewords which James BURTON and Albert LEE agreed to provide. I am both honoured and flattered to reproduce their own words and signature in a Telly book.

Lastly, at the time of closing 8 months of hard work, I want to dedicate this new publication to three important persons who recently passed away: my father, Freddie Tavares and Leo Fender.

A.R. DUCHOSSOIR
July 1991

JAMES BURTON AND THE TELECASTER

I first started playing guitar when I was 13. In 1952, my parents bought me what was to become my perfect guitar — a new Fender Telecaster. I fell in love with it instantly. My style was just developing and I could not have found a better guitar to make that happen. The shape of the neck, the way the guitar balanced and especially the sound was perfect for the way I wanted to play.

It wasn't much longer after I got the guitar that I used it to record "Susie Q" with Dale Hawkins. And that was just the beginning of the recordings that my first Telecaster would appear on. The Rick Nelson hits from 1958 to 1965 were followed by numerous studio dates with artists from Merle Haggard and Buck Owens to Nat King Cole and Frank Sinatra.

In August 1969, Fender sent me the now famous Pink Paisley Telecaster. It first made it on stage with Elvis Presley in Las Vegas. From that day until late 1989, that was my main axe. In 1990, after almost five years of development with Fender, the "James Burton" Signature Model Telecaster was introduced. An almost 40 year love affair with the guitar that got me started has come back to having me put a little bit of myself into the greatest guitar I have ever played.

James Burton

I had been playing guitar for about four years before I touched my first Tele.

I remember walking into a music shop in London and the salesman said "Try this, instant James Burton". James and Jimmy Bryant were and still are favorites of mine and I knew they used Telecasters.

I had enjoyed playing a Gibson but The Tele seemed to embody the term "electric guitar" so much more.

I have never thought of it as an easy guitar to play; raw and unforgiving, but there is a style and feel which the guitar almost channels you to that I think is impossible to duplicate on any other.

My utmost respects to something that has given me so much.

Albert Lee
Malibu '90

ALBERT LEE AND THE TELECASTER

[courtesy Dan Reeder]

5

ACKNOWLEDGEMENTS

The author wishes to extend his thanks to the following people for their contribution to this book.

Pete ALENOV (Pete's Guitar)
Scott ARCH
Margie BAKER (Midwestern Music)
Patrice BASTIEN (Magnetic France)
Bob BENTON (Fender)
Jay BLACK (Fender)
Bill BLACKBURN
George BLANDA (Fender)
Gary BOHANNON
Bruce BOLEN (Fender)
Steve BOULANGER (Fender)
Larry BROOKS (Fender)
Jimmy & Cindy BRYANT
James BURTON
Mike CAROFF (Fender)
Bill CARSON (Fender)
Jonathan CHERRY (Fender)
CHRIS' GUITARS
Jim COLCLASURE (Guitarcheologist)
Didier COLOMBI
Dave CROCKER (Fly by Nite Music)
Jim CRUICKSHANK (Fender)
Vince CUNETTO
Gordon DOW
John ENGLISH (Fender)
Alfredo ESQUIVEL (Fender)
Steve EVANS (Jacksonville Guitar Center)
Yves FARGE
George FULLERTON
Uncle Lou GATANAS
Jeff GRAY
Ted GREENE
George GRUHN (Gruhn Guitars)
George HARRISON
Yasuhiko IWANADE (Fender)

Conrad KISH (Hal Leonard Publishing Corp.)
Susan LANDAU
Albert & Karen LEE
Ron LIRA (Honest Ron's Guitars)
Bill LLOYD (Guitar Preservation)
Seth LOVER
Christophe MADRONNA
John MAHER (Fender)
Keith MARDAK (Hal Leonard Publishing Corp.)
Jacques & Debbie MAZZOLENI
Doug MILLS (Fender)
Albert MOLINARO (Guitars R Us)
Tom MURPHY (Guitar Preservation)
John & Dana PAGE (Fender)
John PEDEN
Eugene ROBERTSON (Eugene's Guitars)
Ricardo RODRIGUEZ (Fender)
Alan ROGAN
Bill SCHULTZ (Fender)
Patrick SELMER
Dan SMITH (Fender)
Richard SMITH
Steve SOEST (Soest's Repair Shop)
Gilbert & Barbara SOUTHWORTH (Southworth Guitars)
John SPRUNG (American Guitar Center)
Mike & Alice STEVENS
Fred STUART (Fender)
Buck & Bucky SULCER (Guitar Network)
Freddie TAVARES
Dave THOMASON (Dave's Guitars)
David WEINSTEIN
Jim WERNER
Jim WILLHITE (Guitar Preservation)
Cliff WILLIAMS
Robert WINGATE

THE ORIGINS OF THE TELECASTER

For a long time the official story has been that the TELECASTER guitar was originally released in 1948 as the BROADCASTER and then renamed in 1950. Over the years that statement was often quoted in the Fender company's literature and more recently a 40th anniversary commemorative model was introduced in 1988 as a limited edition. Although the TELECASTER is indeed the world's first solid body electric produced on a substantial scale (and still a strong contender in today's market), the true origins of the model call for a more accurate account.

FROM LAP STEEL TO SPANISH GUITARS

The FENDER ELECTRIC INSTRUMENT COMPANY was founded in Fullerton, California by Clarence Leo Fender in early 1946 after he amicably separated from Clayton Orr "Doc" Kauffman, his former partner in the short-lived K&F company. The previous year the young K&F Manufacturing Corp. had just built its first Hawaiian guitars and amplifiers a few months before the end of WWII. Leo was keen then to expand the manufacturing activities of K&F, but Doc Kauffman apparently had qualms about the viability of a bigger business in the aftermath of the war and he preferred to pull out from the venture. So Leo Fender set up his own company, continuing the production of lap steels and amps at a time when musicians were deprived of new musical instruments because established manufacturers (like GIBSON) had been diverted into war production work.

Fender lap steels and amps soon gained recognition among professionals and new models were gradually added to expand the line. Although a few were sold through the radio repair shop Leo had set up in 1939, their distribution was handled by a company called RADIO & TELEVISION EQUIPMENT Co. (RTEC). Besides the activities implied by its name, the Santa Ana-based company, owned by Francis Hall, was also marginally involved then in the distribution of musical instruments. In 1946 RTEC became the exclusive distributor of the "Fender Fine Line Electric Instruments." The pattern which would prevail until the CBS take-over in the mid-60s was thus set early on. The Fender company would design and build musical instruments whilst the business side would be handled as a separate operation by its exclusive distributor.

In the late 40s Leo Fender was busy developing new products in Fullerton and RTEC was striving to build up a dealer network. In the beginning its salesmen were confined to Southern California, but Donald Randall, who was RTEC's general manager, soon began to establish dealerships in other states such as Texas. In fact, although his role has often been overshadowed by the stature of Leo Fender in the eye of the public, Donald Randall eventually played a critical part in the worldwide success of Fender instruments through his sales organization. In 1948 RTEC first brought Fender instruments to the annual trade show organized by the NATIONAL ASSOCIATION OF MUSIC MERCHANTS (NAMM). Adverts inviting dealer inquiries were also placed in national trade magazines with a catchy claim reading "Fender for faster turnover - for profit building."

Also in 1948, Leo Fender asked a young man he had met earlier on to work for him and help him out with repairs on amps and lap steels. His name was George Fullerton and, beside participating in the creation of the first Fender electric Spanish guitar, he would become along with Dale Hyatt one of Leo's closest associates and friends in his lifetime. In those days the term "electric Spanish" was used by manufacturers (e.g. Gibson's "ES" prefix) to indicate that the instrument was held in the conventional manner, like a classical Spanish guitar, as opposed to the lap-style of the Hawaiian guitar.

Shortly after he had met Doc Kauffman, Leo Fender had built what was actually his first Spanish guitar, then meant as a test bench for his novel "pickup unit for stringed instruments" with strings through the coil. Because of its odd shape this guitar is often mistaken for a strict lap steel, but it had a round neck and could be used as a Spanish guitar. Both pickup and guitar are featured in the patent jointly filed by Leo and Doc on September 26, 1944 (and granted on December 7, 1948 with number 2,455,575).

Prior to being hired by Leo, George Fullerton remembers he borrowed that guitar: *"I kept it a couple of days and I tried it. It sounded pretty good but it was something you couldn't hold...it was hard to hold. So when I took it back, I told him it sounds pretty neat but it's hard to hold on your lap. He said: well, that's only the beginning!"* (1). The 1944 solid body was primarily intended to test the "direct string pickup" which would later be fitted to the early lap steels made by the Fender Electric Instrument Co. By 1948 Leo Fender began putting together fresh ideas for his first "real" electric Spanish guitar, as recounted by George: *"After I'd been there for a while, we got stranded to come up with this idea of one solid body guitar"* (2).

Looking back some 40 years later, the first Spanish guitar to carry the Fender name was basically rooted in five key concepts.

• It would be EASY TO BUILD, OPERATE AND SERVICE.

In Leo Fender's own words: *"The design of everything we did was intended to be easy to build and easy to repair. When I was in the repair business, dealing with other men's problems, I could see the shortcomings in the design completely disregarding the need for service. If a thing is easy to service, it is easy to build"* (3). Freddie Tavares, who later joined Leo in Spring 1953 and helped with the design of the Stratocaster, confirmed the point: *"Leo Fender's general philosophy, general attitude was make it practical, as practical as possible and as simple as possible"* (4). This pragmatic striving for functionality would illuminate all the products engineered by Leo Fender, without impairing his creative genius.

Besides, in the late 40s, the young Fender company was not in a position to invest in sophisticated tooling equipment simply because it did not have the financial resources to do so. Therefore, necessity being the mother of invention, the new guitar had to be built basically with the equipment already in use for the production of lap steels and amps.

• It would be a SOLID BODY GUITAR.

Spanish electrics had appeared well before WWII but they were all "electrified" acoustic guitars, prone to feedback, with a rather muddy tone. They could not be played too loud and more often than not restricted guitarists to a modest spot in the band (save for Charlie Christian and Oscar Moore of the late 30s). Feedback was the bane of the early electrics. In Leo's own words: *"We wanted to get rid of the feedback that you get with the acoustic guitar [...] We weren't trying to harm the acoustic guitar or anything like that-just come with something that would do a better job for the player"*(5).

So, the new guitar would be built with no acoustic cavity to eliminate feedback which back then was not yet a deliberate aesthetic effect. Additionally, owing to its experience in the production of lap steels, the Fender company was not alien to the wood working involved in the making of solid bodies.

• It would have a DETACHABLE ONE-PIECE NECK.

A detachable neck was not per se a new concept. It had already been used on banjos or by other manufacturers such as Rickenbacher, but not on regular

Spanish guitars. Leo Fender opted for a bolted neck mostly for functional reasons: *"I decided that it'd be best for the customer if I built the body and neck separate. See, a lot of times, even if the neck doesn't have to be replaced- it may just need an adjustment- it's better for the owner just to remove it for shipping. It's much easier than shipping the whole instrument"* (6).

A solid body guitar with a detachable neck was also easier and more economical to produce. This mode of construction would do away with a neck heel and a slight backward angle to the neck, aligned flat with a thinner body. The neck would also be built without a separate glued-on fingerboard and fretted directly. It would entail the use of a good quality hardwood to resist finger-wear, but overall it would be less costly to build or replace.

• It would have a PICKUP WITH INDIVIDUAL POLES.

Sound-wise Leo Fender was keen to retain the tonal characteristics of a lap steel for his Spanish guitar. At that time he was striving to improve his own pickup design, noticeably to obtain a more even string response, and he began experimenting with individual magnet poles. As later recounted in an interview: *"I think that perhaps I was the first person to use separate magnets, one for each string. That way, I found that the notes didn't seem to run together - you could get more of an individual performance off of each string"* (7).

Leo was primarily an electronics man and so he would try out different pickup designs until he found one that sounded right to him. Always in search of functional features, he also made sure that the unit would be adjustable in height to freely modify the balance between treble and bass.

• It would have a FULLY ADJUSTABLE BRIDGE.

Late 40s Spanish guitars were fitted with a pre-set floating bridge made of wood and adjustable in height only.In those days, adjusting string length for intonation implied gently moving the whole bridge unit across the guitar top. Leo Fender was convinced that a "better" Spanish guitar should feature a bridge adjustable both in length and height in order to meet players' needs and requirements.

Back in the late 40s, Leo Fender's intention was to add a solid body electric guitar to his product range. But, from a practical point of view, it basically was conceived as a Spanish version of a lap steel guitar. The rationale was to draw on the sound and type of construction of a lap steel to bring a better guitar to players, in particular to country & western music players. As he would later admit: *"It was from the steel that I got the idea of building a solid version of the Spanish guitar style. Guitarists were always asking about methods of getting more volume and I decided I ought to build something for them!"* (8).

AN ENTIRELY NEW SPANISH GUITAR

In the course of 1949, these ingredients were gradually embodied into a prototype instrument with the assistance of George Fullerton who worked out the body shape: *"I've always been basically into drawing, so I started working to lay out the design for a guitar body, many times until 2 o'clock at night!"*(9). The earliest one-pickup prototype saw the light of day with what would become the classic Telly lines, a simple yet elegant body shape with a deep cutaway that a famous contemporary designer like Charles Eames would not have disavowed. Beyond an almost definitive body design, it incorporated all of the above mentioned key concepts, but it also sported a few transitional features showing that it was only a first draft.

By and large, the most striking feature of the first prototype made in 1949 was without a doubt its lap steel snakehead design with three keys on each side. Back then, Leo had not yet decided upon the asymetric peghead with six in-line tuners on the same side which would later become a trademark for Fender guitars. For practical purposes, the first prototype was thus fitted with two banks of Kluson lap

steel keys. Otherwise, it displays a one-piece maple neck with 21 frets, but a rather large nut width (2"), and position markers were materialized by tiny painted-on black dots.

The body was made of pinewood (not ash) and painted in an opaque white, simply enhanced by a wing-shaped black pickguard covering the lower half of the instrument. The neck was fastened with four bolts via a tempered steel anchor plate, slightly larger (2 5/8" x 1 7/8") than the later production mount. The guitar already displayed the unmistakable bridge pickup assembly, with a slanted pickup, a 3-piece bridge section and string-through-body loading. As later pointed out by the late Freddie Tavares: *"The rear pickup is slanted for a very important reason. That was because when you pluck the instrument way back near the bridge, everything is more brilliant, but you lose the depth. So, the reason for the slant was to get a little more vitality or virility into the bass strings and still maintain all the brilliance"* (10).

The whole assembly was protected by a sliding cover made of a bent metal sheet to provide adequate shielding for the pickup. The jack cup was located on the side of the body, but the volume and tone controls were mounted on a slanted metal plate, almost in the same alignment as the lead pickup. Leo reckoned at first that it would be more practical to have the controls near the guitarist's playing hand, but aesthetics probably lead him to reconsider the argument at a later stage. But both knobs were initially in the same position as the two tone controls of a...Stratocaster! Incidentally, this first prototype (tracked down by well-known dealer and collector, Dave Crocker) still exists today and its (strictly) original pots are dated from the 31st week of 1949, which would indicate that it was completed sometime in Fall of that year. The guitar belongs to its original owner, John Hanley, who received it as a gift from Leo and George once they moved on to the next prototype phase.

The lap steel snakehead was abandoned by late 1949 and replaced by the now classic peghead with all the keys on one side. Leo Fender purportedly drew inspiration from the instruments used by some Croatian musicians he had seen playing in California. Later, he recounted that a string-straight pull to the keys was a prime consideration rather than sheer aesthetic appeal: *"My main reason, though, was that it put all the strings in a straight line to the tuners-right straight through the nut to the peg. I didn't want to fan out the strings like you have to do with pegs on both sides"* (11). It can also be argued that Leo was perhaps influenced to some extent by the headstock of the guitar built in 1947 by Paul Bigsby for Merle Travis in nearby Downey,California. At any rate, the Travis guitar probably confirmed to Leo that it was both a practical and appealing feature. This involved some additional work because the keys then procured from Kluson were not meant to be affixed with only one screw between two shells and the winglets at either end had to be punched with a press.

Development was actively pursued over Winter 1949/1950 and gradually brought in refined appointments such as a slightly narrower neck at the nut, a tone selector switch, a new layout for the controls and a reshaped pickguard. Contrary to what has often been said, the bridge-pickup assembly was patented shortly after it was perfected because Leo Fender was keen to quickly protect his innovative design as he had done with the direct-string pickup unit in 1944. A patent for a "combination and bridge assembly" was thus filed on January 13, 1950 before any Fender electric Spanish guitar was officially introduced. The patent was not fully granted until much later on October 30,1951 (number 2,573,254),but the earliest guitars sold would anyway carry a "PAT.PEND." stamp on the bridge plate. In fact, production models would retain this stamp well after the patent had been effectively granted!

Extracts from the wording of the patent application attest of the functional credo of Leo Fender:

"...the objects of my invention are:

First, to provide a device of this class which [...] incorporates a novel sectional bridge permitting individual adjustment of the strings.

Second, to provide a device of this class wherein the pickup unit may be accurately adjusted relative to the strings of the instrument.

Leo Fender in the late 50s. [courtesy Richard Smith]

Don Randall in the mid-50s.

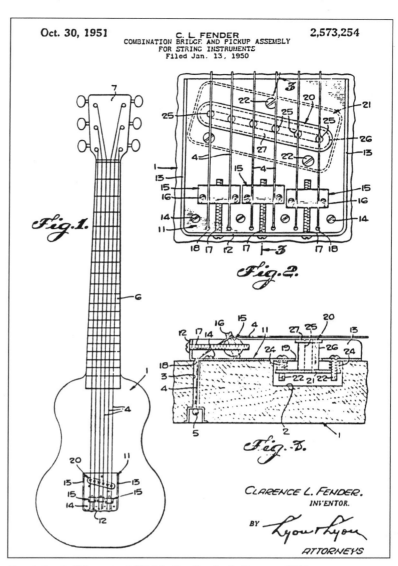

C. L. FENDER
COMBINATION BRIDGE AND PICKUP ASSEMBLY
FOR STRING INSTRUMENTS
Filed Jan. 13, 1950

2,573,254

Fig.1.

Fig.2.

Fig. 3.

CLARENCE L. FENDER.
INVENTOR.

BY Lyon & Lyon
ATTORNEYS

Front sheet of the patent filed by Leo Fender in January 1950.

Details of the first prototype built in 1949. The one-piece maple neck has a lap-steel "snakehead" headstock and is fastened to the body with a 2 5/8" anchor plate. Also note the position of the controls and the wing-shaped black pickguard. Otherwise, the unmistakable body shape and bridge assembly are already there. [courtesy John Hanley/photo by Dave Crocker]

Excerpt from the June 1950 issue of Musical Merchandise.

New Spanish Electric Guitar

● FENDER offers this brand-new Spanish electric guitar, which they call the *"Esquire,"* marketed by Radio & Television Equipment Co., 207 Oak St., Santa Ana, Calif.

The new guitar features a new type one-piece neck (replaceable), new cut-away body, new adjustable bridge and fully-adjustable pick-up. The new neck can be changed by the owner in about 10 minutes, eliminating re-fretting. The cut-away body allows easy playing up to the last fret and has no acoustic cavity to resonate and cause feed-back, the makers state.

In addition to the adjustable pick-up there is a tone-control, with quick tone-change switch. The adjustable bridge permits the player to adjust each string for height and length to meet individual needs.

Finish is in clear maple neck and polished black lacquer body, with white plastic pick guard and all metal parts chrome-plated. Leather strap is included. A case is also available, covered with diagonal-striped linen and crushed-plush lined, with pocket for picks, strings, etc. . . . When writing for more details, you'll mention *Musical Merchandise Magazine*, won't you?

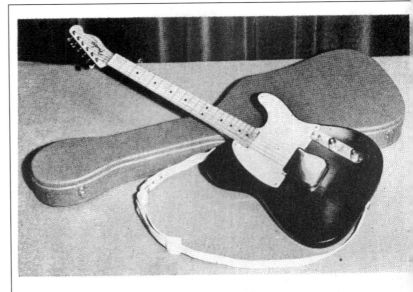

Fender's electric guitar, with solid body.

MUSIC DEALER — CONVENTION SUPPLEMENT 1950

Above: the single pickup black Esquire introduced at the July 1950 NAMM show.

Right: the May 1950 advert featuring Jimmy Wyble with an Esquire. [courtesy Jim Colclasure]

. . . THE SPANISH GUITAR

The Spanish guitar as shown in the 1950 Fender catalogue.

This picture of a dual pickup Esquire was taken by Leo Fender himself. [courtesy Richard Smith]

1950 dual pickup Esquire in blonde
[photo by Kerry Wetzel]

Third, to provide on the whole, a compact assembly which although economical of manufacture and installation is particularly dependable and effective in operation."

To compound the various stages of development, Leo Fender was keen to field-test guitars with working musicians to receive their comments. Many times, Leo and George would go down to clubs at night with a guitar to show it to the featured band over a break between sets. George remembers how they first met Jimmy Bryant in a club called the Riverside Rancho: *"In walks this young fellow, good looking young guy, and he came right over where we were, interested in what we had sitting there. So he picks it up and starts playing it, right back upon the edge of the stage. By then, the band was taking a break from their playing. So this young fellow starts playing on this guitar and finally someone brought an amp over and plugged it in. He was doing some real neat things with it and pretty soon there were a lot of people collected around watching what he was doing. He must have played that guitar two hours by himself...the band finally quit playing and everybody crowded around! It was Jimmy Bryant...our first meeting with Jimmy Bryant. No-one at that time, that I know of at least, could play like Jimmy Bryant"* (12).

George also recounts how Dale Hyatt once took a trip to Northern California with guitars to see if he could get some people interested in the new solid body. He talked some local musicians into trying one of them on stage, but the instrument would not work. So Dale picked up another guitar and it did not play either. George recalls: *"Even the third one wouldn't play and by then they were about ready to throw him [Dale] out. What happened under the pickups, the way we put them together not knowing it, is when the plate was screwed down it was pinching against a wire and eventually cut it and the insulation shorted out!"* (13). Beyond anecdotes such as this, valuable comments and advice were steadily obtained from professional musicians or teachers and helped Leo to fine-tune the specs and appointments of his instruments.

Early in 1950 the basic design was almost completed, but Leo wanted his Spanish guitar to feature two pickups for added versatility. The original single pickup version was at first equipped with a special tone switch to yield a deep rhythm tone in addition to its brilliant natural sound. Ultimately, the idea of a pre-set bassy sound would indeed find its way on both single and dual pickup models. Meanwhile Leo Fender, who was primarily an electronics man, tried various types of coils to come up with a different pickup from the unit so far developed for the lead position. The neck pickup with its characteristic smaller coil was eventually finalized around Spring 1950. For shielding purposes, it was fitted with an encapsulating metal cover held by four pins bent under the bottom plate of the bobbin. After additional dies and tooling were delivered to the factory during the second quarter of 1950, the FENDER ELECTRIC INSTRUMENT Co. was ready to produce a dual pickup electric Spanish guitar. But by April RTEC had decided to introduce a single pickup model for national distribution.

THE ESQUIRE

The single pickup model appeared as the "ESQUIRE" in catalogue No. 2 of Fender Fine Line Instruments published by RTEC in Spring 1950. It was the only Spanish guitar featured in the new catalogue and there was no mention of a possible dual pickup version. Next to a picture of the guitar resting on its case, an abundant literature stressed the novel features of the instrument with phrases such as:

"Something entirely new in the electric Spanish guitar field..."

"Features far in advance of all competition..."

"A new style of construction which vastly improves the usability of this type of instrument..."

"A new type one-piece neck that is more slender and durable..."

"The new adjustable Fender bridge [...] is one of the most important modern guitar developments..."

Its practical advantages were also explicitly described:

"The neck is replaceable and can be changed by the owner in approximately ten minutes time..."

"The guitar can be played at extreme volume without the danger of feedback..."

"The player can adjust each string for height from the fret board and for length, obtaining perfect intonation..."

A couple of weeks later, the Esquire was displayed at the 49th annual NAMM convention held in July 1950 at the Palmer House in Chicago. According to trade magazines from that period (such as *Music Dealer* or *Musical Merchandise*) the single pickup version was the only model officially shown and it listed for $139.95 plus $39.95 for the case.

In retrospect, the most peculiar appointment of the 1950 Esquire is its black-lacquered body trimmed with a white pickguard. In an advert from May 1950 featuring Spade Cooley, Jimmy Wyble holds what appears to be a black Esquire, but the photograph may have been touched-up to match the model described in the catalogue. In the back pages of that same catalogue, a picture of Spade Cooley's Orchestra portrays Jimmy Wyble playing a light-coloured guitar. Other photos of players from the same period as well as the 1950 instruments which have survived to this day tend to confirm that early Fender Spanish guitars were mostly finished in "blonde." Why then a black Esquire in the 1950 catalogue?

By all accounts, Leo Fender certainly preferred the semi-transparent light blonde colour as he probably wanted to capitalize upon the popularity of the limed or pickled finish found on late 40s "modern" furniture. Actually, some lap steels were already produced in Fullerton with a blonde finish before 1950. Besides, although a few early samples were made in pinewood, it was a material too soft and too easily dented for a professional guitar. Therefore, Leo soon switched over to what later catalogues would term a "clear blond hardwood," i.e. ash. Therefore, the black colour might only have come as a suggestion from RTEC, perhaps keen to differentiate the newly introduced Spanish guitar from existing products? Another interesting possibility, though, is that the 1950 Esquire was in fact still *built with a pinewood body*, hence an opaque black lacquer (and a more appealing combination than a straight white finish).

Upon closer examination, the picture found in the 1950 catalogue and trade magazines reveals two peculiar features of the early black Esquire. First, there is no guide on the headstock to hold down the E and B strings. Second, the guitar does not appear to have a 3-position lever switch but rather a push-button, vaguely reminiscent of the "organ button" fitted to Fender lap steels until 1948. At any rate, the 1950 black Esquire is today without contest the rarest specimen in the Telecaster family! This leads to the conclusion that it was certainly never produced in any sizeable quantity and at best two or three samples were made for promotional purposes only. By giving exposure to the single pickup black Esquire, Donald Randall simply intended to put bread on the water...

Meanwhile, although it was not officially announced at the July trade show, a dual pickup version of the Esquire was produced before Summer in Fullerton. If one sample was taken by RTEC to Chicago, it remained behind the scenes. Apparently, Don Randall was of the opinion that the simpler one pickup guitar would – at least initially – prove more attractive and saleable in a market where the amplified music business was still largely in its infancy. On the contrary, Leo Fender preferred the more advanced dual pickup version, of which a few samples were made in limited quantity for direct sale to local musicians. As he later recounted: *"Randall wanted us to come out with the single pickup design and wanted to call it the Esquire. That may be why it showed up in that catalogue and price list and the Broadcaster or the Telecaster didn't. But the Broadcaster was the first one we built"* (14).

For the record, Leo should have stipulated "built in quantity" to validate his statement, because on a purely historical basis the Esquire (whether the single or the dual pickup version) actually came first in 1950. However, neither version was made in any sizeable numbers and both guitars are exceedingly rare today, although some two-pickup Esquires have been documented. Compared to later production

models, they can be primarily identified by:

- a one-piece maple neck without a reinforcing truss rod, i.e. without an adjusting bolt at the heel
- a body without a small channel between the neck pocket and the rhythm pickup cavity.

They are also characterized by a headstock decal with a silver Fender "spaghetti" logo, no string guide on the peghead (although original owners often had it added later), steel bridge sections, a tin bottom plate on the lead pickup and of course slot-head screws everywhere. As a rule, there are no date markings to be found on the neck or the body and the only element likely to help with their vintage is the pot code (e.g. 137006 = February 1950 on the pictured Esquire #0013). Judging from the very few samples available today, most of them were made with an ash body and finished in blonde with a contrasting black pickguard. Lastly, they come in a symmetrical form-fit case, usually branded inside the pocket with a small label reading "Bulwin Mfg.Co. Costa Mesa Calif." The earliest Bulwin cases feature a diagonal-stripe linen or a leather-style dark brown covering with a red lining.

At any rate, the argument between Leo Fender and Don Randall about the pickup outfit of the new electric Spanish guitar was quickly overshadowed by a more nagging question raised during the July 1950 trade show.

THE BROADCASTER

It is fair to say that the Fender Spanish guitar displayed at the 1950 Chicago convention did not cause an overnight sensation. Don Randall and Charles Hayes, who were in attendance at the RTEC booth, perhaps did not expect to take huge orders but at least they could hope to test the reaction of dealers and competitors. The latter were quite prone to make joking comments about the new instrument, calling it a "plank," a "toilet seat with strings" or a "canoe paddle!"

On a more serious note, it was soon pointed out that the neck of the new guitar did not have a reinforcing truss rod. This device, first perfected by Gibson-employee Thaddeus McHugh in the early 20s, was then found (whether adjustable or not) on most professional guitars. Don Randall promptly realized that it would be unrealistic to try to sell a professional guitar, even of a radically novel design, without a reinforcing truss rod. Upon his return to California after the show, he proceeded to raise the issue with Leo Fender.

Until Summer 1950 the Spanish guitars built by Leo Fender were all fitted with a rather chunky one-piece maple neck with a pronounced V-shape. Leo was convinced that a hard rock maple neck was strong enough to counterbalance string pressure without a reinforcing truss rod. To prove his point, legend has it that he had one neck tested at the factory by having someone stand on it while it was placed between two chairs. So Leo Fender initially disagreed with Randall when the latter told him it would be a good idea to install a truss-rod into the neck.

A few weeks of indecision ensued and rumour has it that this bone of contention threw a temporary wedge into the relationship between Leo and his distributor. During that period, the electric Spanish guitar was momentarily put on the backburner and the emphasis swung back to lap steels and amps, then in growing demand. A very few 2-pickup models without a truss rod (and possibly any headstock decal) were sold directly from the factory to help with the cash-flow of the company, but their number was insignificant by any standards.

As the late Freddie Tavares once recalled: *"Leo had a knack of thinking slowly and consecutively – no flashes of genius – a merciless unstoppable slow degree of thinking"*(15). This may be why Leo Fender ultimately changed his mind and decided to go ahead with a built-in truss rod. Taking into account Leo's general attitude vis-à-vis the suggestions of musicians, it may well be that a few professional players acquainted with the Fullerton factory did in fact persuade him of the merits of Randall's point of view. Or perhaps one of his early necks failed and warped. Anyway, Leo did change his mind but he also managed to convince Donald Randall that the 2-pickup model was a more appropriate product to break new ground in the market.

By Fall 1950, the Fender dual pickup electric Spanish guitar was officially introduced for national distribution under the "Broadcaster" designation at a $169.95 list price (plus $39.95 for the Bulwin form-fit case). Since the July trade show, the Esquire designation was mostly associated with the single pickup model and it was therefore decided to give a new name to the "new" two-pickup guitar. As later recalled by Don Randall: *"For Leo Fender's first smash guitar, I thought and thought about what to call it. I finally decided to use something that had to do with broadcasting. I named it Broadcaster"* (16). It was a smart name to convey the modernity of the new instrument at a time when music was so dependant on "broadcasts" (radio or television) to thrive and reach the public.

To accompany the release of the Broadcaster, a fact-packed 8.5"x 11" colour insert was placed in trade magazines and served as an additional catalogue sheet. Headlined "NEW FENDER ELECTRIC STANDARD" with Broadcaster in the upper right-hand corner, it showed the instrument in perspective along with four additional shots for close-ups and details. The many novel features of the guitar were duly described and itemized in boxed captions. Both FENDER and RTEC were convinced they had a radically innovative product and it was time to move ahead fast to turn it into a commercial success. The single pickup Esquire was temporarily put aside to allow for the Fender company to concentrate on the production of the Broadcaster.

Unlike the previous non truss-rod Esquire, the Broadcaster was made in larger quantities, hence its claim to be truly the world's first solid body electric produced on a substantial scale. Having said that, numbers should be put in perspective. In 1950 a total of a quarter million guitars was sold in the United States, including a large number of ukuleles. Electric Spanish guitars were not yet produced in great numbers and a more senior company like Gibson barely made 1400 electrics during that year. The actual number of Broadcasters made remains subject to controversy, with quoted estimates ranging from 50 to 500 or more. Bearing in mind the tooling equipment and the workforce of the Fullerton factory in late 1950, it seems doubtful that more than 200 Broadcasters were actually made during the six months or so that the model lasted. Besides, the United States had just entered into the Korean war (on June 30, 1950) and restrictions on materials like steel,copper and aluminium were gradually enforced for the production of most consumer durable goods. This may explain why, for instance, FENDER was having difficulties early on in procuring tuners from Kluson.

Compared to the previous 2-pickup Esquire, the Broadcaster is characterized by a one-piece maple neck with an adjustable truss-rod. Owing to the method of installing the reinforcing rod (i.e. from the rear), the neck has a visible wood fill on the back spine (a.k.a. "skunk stripe") and above the nut. On some of the earliest Broadcasters, however, Fender used maple -for cosmetic purposes- to fill in the truss-rod routings. At a distance, these guitars may look as if they were not fitted with a truss rod, like the earlier Esquire models.

Otherwise, the ash-bodied Broadcaster has a small channel routed between the neck pocket and the rhythm pickup cavity to permit truss-rod adjustment. A round string-guide is screwed on the headstock next to the Fender silver "spaghetti" logo and the bridge saddles are made of brass. All the screws, including the truss-rod bolt" have a slotted cap. Lastly, although a few early Broadcasters may not feature any date markings on the neck or the body,most of them do.With a regular production now underway, Fender employees began in October 1950 to pencil dates on both neck and body.

Whilst both FENDER and RTEC were gearing up to make a success of the new solid body electric, they suddenly had to discontinue the use of the Broadcaster designation.

THE TELECASTER

In early 1951 the "Broadcaster" name was dropped following a request from the FRED.GRETSCH Mfg. Co. The New-York-based company was marketing a series of drums under a similar designation, albeit with a slightly different spelling ("Broadkaster"). GRETSCH wrote to RTEC in February 1951 to stress that they already owned the trademark for the Broadcaster name. In those days, GRETSCH was a well established name in the music industry and a much bigger business than FENDER. Besides, RTEC was keen to maintain good relationships with other

In the early days, country & western bands were Fender's strongest advocates. The Silver Spur Boys portrayed here display an impressive array of Fender Fine Electric Instruments, including one single and two dual pickup electric Spanish guitars. *[courtesy John Peden]*

The Broadcaster insert printed to complement the 1950 catalogue in the latter part of the year. *[courtesy Jim Colclasure]*

1950 Broadcaster resting on a Dual Professional amp. *[photo by John Peden]*

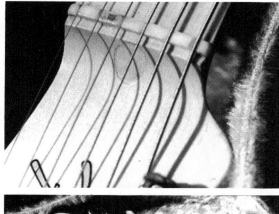

Broadcaster headstock. Note the maple plug near the nut. *[photos by John Sprung]*

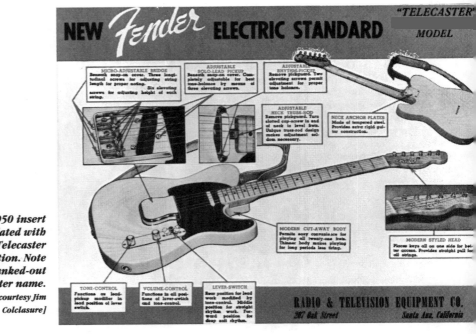

*1951
Telecaster
[photo by
Steve Evans]*

*The 1950 insert
updated with
a Telecaster
designation. Note
the blanked-out
Broadcaster name.*
*[courtesy Jim
Colclasure]*

*The "No-Caster"
headstock with
clipped-off
Broadcaster
name. [courtesy
Jeffrey Gray]*

*The patent filed by Leo
Fender in April 1951 to
protect the innovative
design of his solid body
Spanish electric guitar.*

Aug. 14, 1951   C. L. FENDER   Des. 164,227
GUITAR
Filed April 23, 1951

FIG. 1.   FIG. 2.   FIG. 3.

CLARENCE L. FENDER,
INVENTOR.
BY
Lyon & Lyon
ATTORNEYS.

1951 TELECASTER SPECIFICATIONS

NECK
- one-piece detachable hard rock maple neck
- fully adjustable reinforcement metal truss rod
- 4-bolt mounting on to the body with tempered steel anchor plate
- asymetric peghead with straight string pull to the tuners
- round string guide on peghead to press down E and B strings
- 25.5" scale length
- 21 nickel silver frets
- 7.25" fretboard radius
- 1.625" nut width
- black dot position markers

BODY
- thin solid-body construction
- figured ash body
- original deep cutaway for convenient access to all 21 frets
- neck-to-body junction near 16th fret
- string-through-body loading for improved sustain
- dimensions= 15.75" (length) x 12" (width) x 1.75" (depth)

PICKUPS & CONTROLS
- 2 original single-coil pickups with distinct specifications for the bridge and neck positions
- each pickup with 6 individual Alnico magnets and polepieces
- each pickup fully adjustable in height
- lead pickup (42GA wire) with DC resistance of ca. 7.5kOhms
- conveniently slanted for improved output
- rhythm pickup (43GA wire) with DC resistance of ca. 7.7kOhms
- 3-position selector switch for different tone settings
- master volume control
- pan control to combine both pickups for added versatility
- side-mounted jack receptacle

HARDWARE
- 6 Kluson Deluxe tuning keys with slotted headpost
- 2-way adjustable bridge section (height and length) with three individual brass saddles
- snap-on bridge cover
- single-ply black pickguard with 5 mounting screws
- chrome-plated brass knobs with heavy knurl for better grip
- nickel-plated strap buttons

FINISH
- neck: sealed with clear nitro-cellulose lacquer
- body: semi-transparent blonde lacquer

ACCESSORIES
- brown form-fit hard case with golden brown plush lining
- adjustable leather strap plus shielded cord and polishing cloth

manufacturers and a dispute over the Broadcaster trademark would not have done any good to the reputation of Fender instruments. This is why Don Randall opted for the immediate discontinuation of the Broadcaster name on the Fender Spanish guitar. A new designation had to be found...

In the very early 50s, television was quickly becoming the new craze in the United States. In 1951 six million receivers were already in use and more than 5 million units would be manufactured during the same year, despite the restrictions entailed by the Korean war. Additionally, many people felt that the development of television greatly benefitted the music industry as a whole, as emphasized by William Gard, then executive secretary of the NAMM: *"The mid century's wonder medium, television, has had a most beneficial effect on the sale of musical instruments"* (17).

Aptly enough, it did not take long for Don Randall to blend television into Broadcaster and coin the "Telecaster" name. However, in order to avoid another mishap with the new designation, RTEC took care to have a trademark search conducted prior to putting the new name in print on the Fender Spanish guitar. In April 1951 the Telecaster name was cleared and shortly thereafter first appeared in Fender adverts placed by RTEC in trade magazines. The 8.5" x 11" colour insert previously used to describe the dual pickup guitar was modified and the Telecaster name printed above a blanked-out Broadcaster designation.

The hiccup with the Broadcaster name did not stop production of electric Spanish guitars at the Fullerton factory. Upon receipt of the GRETSCH request, Leo Fender simply clipped the disputed name off the headstock decal. For a period of time, dual pickup models were thus produced with only the Fender brandname on the peghead. This transitional feature should theoretically have lasted until the new "Telecaster" trademark had been cleared for public use, but Leo Fender was not a man to waste anything. The Fender factory kept on using clipped Broadcaster decals until it ran out of them around August 1951.

The '51 guitars with only the Fender name on the headstock have since earned a number of nicknames among which the most commonly accepted today is the "No-Caster." Technically, this nickname is in no way a legitimate Fender designation but it has gained a quasi-official status among collectors and Fender afficionados as a whole. As a transition model, the earlier No-Casters are actually similar to Broadcasters in most respects whilst the later ones share the same features as the first (properly labelled) Telecasters (i.e. top rout between the two pickups or shorter control knobs). Barring a few minor cosmetic details, the Broadcaster, the No-Caster and the early Telecaster made in 1951 are essentially the same electric guitar. They feature the same typical wiring circuit without a "real" tone control and their 3-position pickup selector switch works as follows:

- forward position: neck pickup alone with a pre-set bassy sound and no tone control (i.e. "deep soft rhythm")
- middle position: neck pickup alone with a normal sound, but no tone control (i.e. "straight rhythm work")
- rear position: both pickups together with the neck pickup gradually "blended" into the lead pickup according to the setting of the so-called tone control (i.e. "lead work").

This specific wiring would be modified only in 1952.

Beside the Telecaster name, the other aftermath of the Broadcaster hiccup with GRETSCH was to induce Leo Fender to properly register the innovative design of his electric Spanish guitar. The patent for a "new, original and ornamental design for a guitar" was filed on April 23, 1951 and granted on August 14, 1951 under number Des. 164,227. It was not mentioned in the application wording that the said design was for a solid body guitar, but the accompanying drawings were explicit enough in this respect.

Early in the year, FENDER and RTEC also resurrected the single pickup Esquire to complement the Spanish guitar offering. Technically, the two versions were only differentiated by their pickup outfit and relevant wiring circuit (albeit with a similar-looking 3-position tone switch on both guitars). Otherwise, the 1951 Esquire was produced with exactly the same body and neck as the dual pickup model, including a routed cavity for the "missing" neck pickup. Price wise, the dual pickup model

then listed for $189.50 whilst the Esquire was going for $149.50. Both guitars were available with a $39.95 form-fit case, featuring after mid-51 a light brown alligator covering with golden brown lining.

A $40 gap hardly reflected the actual difference in cost price of the two instruments, especially if one bears in mind that the Telecaster rhythm pickup was soon listed as a replacement part for $21! In other words, Fender (or RTEC) was not applying the same mark-up to both guitars. Whatever the pricing formula, the rationale developed by RTEC then was to widen the price range between the two models in order to skim more efficiently the budding market for electric Spanish guitars. Initially, it worked fine, even though the Esquire would be produced over the years in smaller numbers than the Telecaster.

Compared to the version tentatively offered in 1950, the new Esquire was fitted with a wiring circuit meant to emulate the tonal possibilities of the more expensive dual pickup guitar. A similar 3-position was used to provide the following settings:

- forward position: pre-set bassy sound
- middle position: normal pickup sound with a real tone control
- rear position: lead sound and no tone control with the pickup directly wired to the output jack.

Combined with the specifications of the early 50s Fender pickups, this wiring has turned some of the early Esquires into the best screamers ever made in Fullerton!

In July 1951 both the Telecaster and the Esquire were displayed at the annual NAMM trade show organized in Chicago. Accordingly, the 1950 Broadcaster insert was updated for a third time with the two models name and featured in the main trade magazines released for the convention. Despite the pinch in consumer goods because of the Korean war, Leo Fender and Don Randall were confident that their solid body electric Spanish guitars had a bright future. However, they certainly did not envisage that forty years later the Telecaster would still be one of the most revered solid body electrics! In 1951, the wheels were definitively set in motion for radical changes not only in the guitar field, but also in the music industry as a whole.

40 YEARS OF TELECASTERS
AN OVERVIEW

Since 1951 Telecaster guitars have been produced in many variants, which sometimes differ by more than simple cosmetic appointments or specific manufacturing idiosyncrasies. Some of them only have in common the name and the overall body shape. Over the last 40 years, there is not just one model to be accounted for but several. To recap their whereabouts, this overview has been divided according to the three major periods in the Fender history: the Leo Fender years, the CBS years and the more recent "post-CBS" era.

THE LEO FENDER YEARS
1951-1964

THE EARLY BLACK GUARD TELLIES

Both the Telecaster and the Esquire kept their basic 1951 appointments until the mid-50s. In retrospect, their most striking features – at least cosmetically speaking – are a typical yellowed blonde finish (a.k.a. "butterscotch" finish) and a black pickguard, hence the often-cited notion of early "black guard" Tellies. The combination of the two actually gives a distinct look to the early 50s models, which are otherwise considered by many as the ultimate classic Telecaster guitar because of their tone. This also explains why the "vintage" Telecaster introduced by FENDER in the early 80s is a '52 reissue.

Besides its peculiar hue, the original blonde finish nicely showcases the ash body heavy grain pattern that later whiter finishes would subdue. More often than not, the early 50s bodies are thought of as being one piece but this is not the case. They are usually made of two-pieces – sometimes three – and rarely one, painstakingly bookmatched and adequately painted at the factory to look like one board.

Prior to mid-54, the only major evolution dealt with the Telecaster wiring circuit which was modified by Leo Fender in 1952. The second control, originally construed as a "blender" or a "pan control," was turned into a real tone control as on the Esquire. Conversely, this modification prohibited any two-pickup combination since Leo retained the pre-set boomy tone selected in the switch forward position. The 2nd generation of black guard Telecaster thus has a tone control, but it is functional only in the middle (neck p.u.) and rear (bridge p.u.) switch positions. This circuit provides what catalogue then termed "short duration rhythm tone," "full concert tone" and "lead or take-off tone."

On a more utilitarian note, it was also in 1952 that the symmetrical form-fit case with a bulb at the top end was replaced by a flat-sided brown case (a.k.a. "poodle case"), probably on practical grounds.

The 1951 NAMM show had definitely put the solid body electric on the map and demonstrated FENDER's leading edge in this field, but life was not that easy then for US musical instruments manufacturers. The nagging ulcer of the time was Korea. By October 1st, the Controlled Materials Plan had imposed further restrictions on the non-defense use of critical metals such as steel, copper or aluminium. The editorial of the September 1951 issue of *Musical Merchandise* reflected pessimistic comments like "Most everyone agrees that there will be scarcities in the future – and this includes musical instruments which contain critical materials." Simultaneously, inflation and raised taxes were hurting consumers' pockets and their disposable income.

The impact of the Korean war did not prevent FENDER from shortly outrunning production capacity. With an armistice in sight by mid-53, fretted instruments manufacturers found themselves, according to *Music Trades Magazine*, "unable to cope with unforeseen increase in demand this Spring." In early 1953, FENDER acquired a 3 1/2 acre tract in East Fullerton to erect three new manufacturing

buildings. Besides, the success of Fender instruments as a whole was such that it had outgrown the services of RTEC, still involved in radio and electronic devices. A new company called FENDER SALES, Inc. was therefore set-up by the associated parties and took over the distribution of Fender products as of June 1, 1953. Headquartered in Santa Ana like RTEC, it simply incorporated the existing marketing staff in a fully dedicated organisation and kept the same sales reps in all territories. At first FENDER SALES was equally owned by Don Randall, president, Leo Fender, Francis Hall (owner of RTEC) and Charlie Hayes (sales supervisor of the Fender division of RTEC). However, after the latter was killed in a car accident in June 1955, Francis Hall was bought out by Don and Leo who then remained sole equal partners in FENDER SALES.

With an enlarged factory and a fully dedicated marketing organisation, sales were expected to rise by almost 100% within the next six months. Spurred by catchy slogans such as "Give yourself that extra playing advantage – Buy a Fender instrument now!" or "Don't cheat yourself by not trying the remarkably outstanding instruments produced by Fender" sales were indeed growing rapidly. Amplified music as a whole was making big strides in the nifty 50s and the solid body concept was more and more readily accepted, with manufacturers like GIBSON or VALCO ("National") joining the bandwagon.

In the mid-fifties, Country & Western players were still the main, but not the sole, advocates of Fender electrics. The transition from traditional Southern blues to an electrified modern idiom in cities like Chicago or Detroit created new opportunities for Fender instruments. Often dubbed "the father of Chicago blues," manish boy McKinley Morganfield alias MUDDY WATERS soon adopted the Telecaster as his perennial companion for slide guitar playing. Other blues artists like BB KING or Clarence "Gatemouth" BROWN also fell then for the blonde solid bodies from Fullerton. However, the first a long series of "Telecaster heroes" was undoubtedly the amazing Jimmy BRYANT, who soon became one of FENDER's featured Telly endorsers along with Alvino REY, Arthur SMITH and Jimmy DOYLE.

A SPATE OF NEW APPOINTMENTS

1954 is generally acknowledged as the year of the Stratocaster, but it also marks the beginning of a number of changes in the appointments of Telecaster guitars. By Fall, the bakelite black guard was replaced by a single ply white trim and a few months later steel superseded brass for the bridge saddles. FENDER also changed the finishing process of the blonde finish, as implied by the distinctive looks of the post-54 Telecasters and Esquires available today. The typical "butterscotch" colour gave way to a creamier shade which would soon evolve into a lighter off-white finish. Finally, 1954 is also the year when the serial number was removed from the bridge plate to be stamped on the neck anchor plate.

At the same time, a stronger (and prettier) protection was made available for Fender guitars with the inception of new oblong "tweed" hard cases (i.e. covered with "airplane luggage linen"). The early tweed case with a centre pocket and a neck support was used for about a year. After mid-55 the inner fittings were modified and the pocket was moved in the lower left-hand corner. A plastileather padded bag also became available in 1954 as a more economical alternative.

Beyond these cosmetic features, a more dramatic evolution took place in 1955. The bridge pickup was modified to incorporate staggered pole pieces in place of the flush level-poles of the original design. The research carried out to perfect the Stratocaster pickups probably triggered this modification to remedy what Leo Fender considered then as a major shortcoming in his early pickup: an imbalanced string response. After Summer 1955 the bridge pickup was built with staggered pole pieces and contrary to popular belief, flush poles pickup were retained for about a year after the discontinuation of black guards.

The first Telecaster hero: virtuoso guitarist Jimmy Bryant. As recalled by George Fullerton: "No-one at that time could play like Jimmy Bryant!" [courtesy Albert Lee]

The advert used by Radio-Tel in 1951-52 [courtesy Jim Colclasure]

Clarence "Gatemouth" Brown posing with a black guard Telly in the early 50s.

1953 Telecaster with matching "poodle case" [courtesy Robert Wingate]

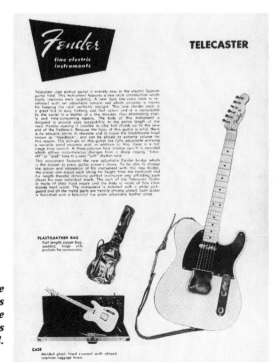

One of the Telecaster pages featured in the 1956 dealer's service manual.

A young Blues Boy King with an early 50s Esquire. [photo courtesy of Michael Ochs Archives]

17

The Johnny Burnette Rock 'n' Roll Trio featuring Paul Burlison with a white guard Esquire. [photo courtesy of Michael Ochs Archives]

Roy Nichols, long time member of Merle Haggard's Strangers, on stage in the 80s. [photo by Yves Farge]

1957 Esquire in 2-tone sunburst. [courtesy Pete Alenov]

Late 50s Telecaster adverts from the "You won't part with yours either" campaign run by Fender Sales for about a decade.

1955 Telecaster resting on a centre-pocket tweed case. [photo by Patrick Selmer]

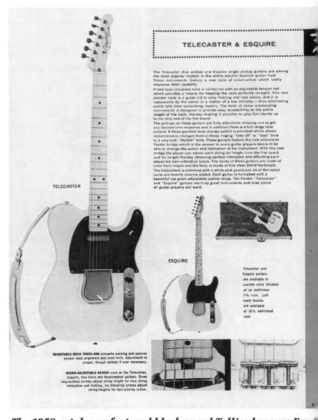

The 1958 catalogue featured black guard Tellies because Fender Sales reckoned they would show up better in black and white.

Finally, the round clubby neck of the post-1950 guitars evolved into a pronounced "V" feel by 1955 and until early 1958 "boat necks" were the rule on most Fender instruments. The heavy dome knobs were replaced by much lighter flat top knobs during 1956 and the small barrel switch tip also gave way to a bigger top-hat design. At the end of 1956, Telecaster guitars no longer looked or even sounded exactly the same as the 1951 models.

Meanwhile, business was extremely buoyant for FENDER at the leading edge of the amplified music boom. More dealerships were being won by Don Randall's far-sighted prophesy: *"The amplified music business is still in its infancy, its surface has only been scratched, its possibilities practically unlimited. Retailers taking full advantage of the current and ever-increasing interest in electric instruments not only build present volume sales, but firmly establish themselves in a market which promises great future profit potential"* (18). FENDER SALES soon developed a heavy merchandising including store banners, window streamers, photos of artist endorsers, display stands, advertising mats and curtains not to forget glossier catalogues and folders.

At the July 1955 NAMM show, Don Randall was quoted in *Down Beat Magazine* as saying that "Fender is having a hard time keeping up with demand for electric guitars." With new products added to the range every year, the manufacturing side had somewhat lagged behind the creative spirit of Leo Fender and the marketing skills of Don Randall. As early as 1954, an industrial engineer named Forrest White was hired by Leo to address this critical issue. Officially appointed plant manager in 1955, Forrest White set out to completely reorganize the manufacturing activities of Fullerton.

A more efficient plant operation was necessary because the market turned into a different ball game with the birth of Rock and Roll. A whole new generation of players burst onto the scene and, whether amateur or professional, they more often than not chose Fender electric instruments to rock along. Among them, a young man called James BURTON, who had just recorded Suzie Q with Dale Hawkins at the age of 16, would soon become a cult figure in the Telecaster realm and more simply as a musician.

Rock and roll also propped up the advent of "custom-coloured" guitars, which so far only a handful of country players had been keen to request directly from Leo Fender at the factory. In a rather conservative environment mesmerized by the Cold War, playing a red guitar was not exactly fashionable! By 1956, though, special paint jobs in colours of the player's choice became available at an additional 5% charge. Later, FENDER would propose its own selection of custom colours derived from automotive paints. As recalled by George Fullerton: *"No-one was making coloured instruments back then, so it was an opportunity for us to do something different and it turned out pretty nice"* (19).

This option, however, was not exercised then by many players and 50s Telecaster guitars with a custom finish are exceedingly rare, but a few are known to exist and have been documented. In 1957-58, a few samples were also produced with the same 2-tone sunburst as the Stratocaster or the Precision Bass. Although sunburst was not a special finish per se at factory level, it was then a true custom colour for Telecasters and Esquires, otherwise finished in blonde as standard production models.

Both models underwent few significant modifications until mid-59, with the notable exception of string loading. By Fall 1958, the original string-through-body pattern was discontinued in favour of a "top loading" bridge. This probably saved the factory time (and money) by not having to drill the body nor to install back ferrules. The new outfit – already applied to the P.Bass in mid-57 – did not, however, prove too successful on Telecaster guitars and FENDER reverted to the original stringing pattern in late 1959.

In the course of 1958, necks gradually changed for a flatter cross section whilst late 50s Fender instruments usually show cleaner tooling marks, reflecting newer jigs and fixtures compared to previous years. Despite the pictures in the 1957 and 1958 catalogues, a black guard trim was not reinstated in the late 50s. FENDER SALES simply realized that blonde Tellies with a white guard did not come out too

well in black and white pictures (e.g. 1955 catalogue). Therefore a few black guards were unearthed and fixed on late 50s guitars to provide more attractive catalogue shots even though the accompanying description specifies that "the instrument is trimmed with a white pickguard!"

By 1959, four additional buildings were completed to expand the Fullerton operation whose total production area now extended over approximately 54,000 sq.ft. The Fender company had snowballed during the 50s and employed well over a hundred people at the close of the decade. In Spring, Leo Fender appointed Forrest White as vice-president and general manager, whilst George Fullerton became vice-president in charge of production.

THE ADVENT OF ROSEWOOD FRETBOARD

1959 is a turning point in the early history of Telecaster guitars. It is the year when the original one-piece maple neck was (temporarily) discontinued and replaced by a more conventional 2-piece neck with a separate rosewood fretboard. The Jazzmaster, introduced at the July 1958 NAMM show, was the first Fender electric offered with a rosewood fretboard. This new trim originated in a commercial request from FENDER SALES, as recounted by Freddie Tavares: *"Our distributors, which were a different entity, would come up from time to time with suggestions because they had their ideas and thoughts on marketing. They wanted a rosewood fingerboard. They said: everybody else has one, why can't we have one?"* (20).

They did get one but in 1959, however, it was decided to shift all guitars to rosewood-capped necks. Such a radical evolution was probably brought about by problems of wear on the clear-lacquered maple necks as well as the positive reaction of dealers vis-à-vis the new Jazzmaster neck. At any rate, by Summer 1959, Telecaster guitars were produced with rosewood-capped necks.

Fender successively tried different types of rosewood cap. The earliest variant, found until mid-1962, is milled flat on the neck, hence its usual "slab board" nickname because of a thicker layer of rosewood. The factory then opted for a thinner pre-contoured board which by mid-63 finally looked more like a veneer. The rationale behind these successive combinations was to strike the best compromise between rosewood and maple, so that both timbers would not over-react when glued together. Rosewood is denser and this is why the thickness of the fretboard was ultimately reduced.

The move towards a rosewood cap entailed a change in the installation of the truss rod, no longer inserted from the rear but from the front prior to glueing the fretboard to the neck base. It also brought about a modification in the headstock radius behind the nut. Having said that, the earliest rosewood neck prototypes were built with a rear truss rod installation, hence the presence of a walnut plug above the nut as seen in '59 catalogues. Finally, in line with comtemporary industry trends, the rosewood fingerboard signalled the inception of Fender necks with a much flatter cross-section.

Coincidentally, the abandoning of the one-piece maple neck also marked the withdrawal of "tweed" cases. The luggage linen covering was replaced by Tolex, a more durable vinyl fabric made by the General Tyre & Rubber Co. In 1959, cases first came out fitted with a brown Tolex covering, later changed to white (1963) and finally black (1965).

Beside the advent of rosewood fretboard, the June 1959 NAMM convention held in New York saw the debut of the TELECASTER and ESQUIRE CUSTOM. Intended as a deluxe version of the regular models, they were characterized by what Fender called "the custom treatment of the body," i.e. a sunburst finish with a contrasting white binding and a triple-ply white pickguard.

Otherwise, with the exception of an alder body, their basic appointments were identical to the mid-59 "standard" Telecaster and Esquire models. It would appear, however, that the rosewood board neck was initially conceived as an integral part of the "custom treatment" before the decision was taken to extend this new trim to the entire range of electrics. In a letter to its dealers before the show, FENDER SALES stressed that "these two models fill the requests of many

dealers," which may partly explain the switch to classier rosewood necks for all Fender guitars. Additionally, it could be said that the Custom variants were also an attempt to revisit the 10-year old Telecaster concept with a touch of Gibson looks!

The sunburst finish with a contrasting binding caused Fender a few headaches in the beginning. Although they look today as if they were finished with a 2-tone sunburst, the early Customs were actually sprayed with a 3-tone shading. But, owing to chemical reaction, the red stain usually faded away after being exposed to daylight. Something was probably wrong in the colour pigments FENDER used then on sunburst finishes and the factory did experiments to trace the problem. As recalled by Bill Carson: *"We had to search and so we sprayed many blocks of alder and put them on the top of the building to see which ones would fade and which ones wouldn't! The red just simply got gobbled up in this chemical interaction"* (21). By 1961, though, FENDER finally managed to obtain a lasting 3-tone sunburst. The factory also experienced teething troubles to keep the white binding properly glued to the body edge and it had to seek advice from MARTIN to learn the right procedure.

Initially, the triple ply pickguard of the new Custom guitars was fastened with five screws, but production models quickly received eight screws for a tighter mount. Compared to single ply units, the early triple deckers have a distinct greenish tint, often attributed to ageing. In fact, this peculiar feature originates in the nitrate material used then by the factory, and even when brand new these 3-ply guards never looked pure white. From 1959 they were also fitted on custom-coloured Telecaster guitars, whilst the standard models kept a single ply unit, albeit mounted with eight screws.

During the early 60s, custom colours came to the fore and truly became an integral part of the Fender style. The new 1960 catalogue displayed a Telecaster in "DuPont Red finish," but the following year FENDER would release its own selection of custom colours. The first chart appeared in 1961 with 14 optional finishes available at a 5% additional cost. Besides, Blond (the final "e" fell out after 1959) was still a standard finish on regular Telecasters but a custom option on other models, whilst Sunburst came standard on the newer Custom models, but was a chargeable option on regular Telecaster guitars.

The ensuing catalogues abounded with gorgeous automotive finishes, frequently displayed on guitars other than Telecasters. Apart from one sample in Fiesta Red, Telecaster models were mostly featured in the more classic Blond and Sunburst, probably because FENDER SALES was keen to retain an all-around appeal to the instrument. In the early 60s, the company's senior solid body was still a strong marketing asset, but it was otherwise considered a rather plain guitar compared to the fancier Jaguar or Jazzmaster. Cases too were fancier and an optional rust-coloured molded case, made of high impact vacuum-formed styrene and fitted with gold anodized stripping, was first listed (for $75) in the No. 2 issue of *Fender Facts*, the company's gazette.

In 1963, though, FENDER enlarged its Telly offering and introduced an optional red mahogany body on the regular models. Although it was prominently featured in mid-60s catalogues, the MAHOGANY TELECASTER – perhaps conceived as an answer to Gibson's red SG guitars – was not produced in great numbers and was ultimately discontinued after 1965. By the end of 1963, a triple-ply pickguard was also fitted to the regular Blond models to enhance their looks. Telecasters and Esquires kept a nitrate "green guard" until about early 1965, when the highly inflammable material was finally replaced by straight white plastic.

New music styles had burst onto the scene and contributed to expanding FENDER's clientele. This was the surf era, with the BEACH BOYS and their like celebrating the pleasures of suntanned beach parties and hot-rod racing in Southern California. The advert claim was then "Fender makes music to surf by" and also bright-coloured fancy guitars to go by. The rather plain Telecaster and Esquire were not that popular with surfers, who usually preferred the off-waist contoured lines of other Fender guitars.

Although they were probably produced in fewer numbers than other Fender models during the early 60s, Telecaster guitars nevertheless enjoyed strong

exponents. A myriad of American guitarists avidly watched on TV the Adventures of Ozzie and Harriet between 1958 and 1965 to steal the licks of James BURTON backing Rickie Nelson. At the same time, Buck OWENS and Don RICH were acting naturally with Tellies and both Merle HAGGARD and Roy NICHOLS were no strangers to the model. In Memphis, the STAX recording sessions were branded with the unmistakable choked rhythm patterns of Steve CROPPER, featured guitarist with Booker T. and the MG's and prominent figure in a long list of R&B Telly players.

Meanwhile, Europe was getting to grips with the Stratocaster legend via the Shadows and preparing itself for Beatlemania, but Telecasters were not yet in great demand across the Atlantic, except in the heart of a young English virtuoso named Albert LEE.

By 1964, the success of Fender products as a whole was such that the FENDER ELECTRIC INSTRUMENT Co. had grown into one of the major corporations in the music industry, if not the biggest in terms of volume. The Fullerton factory then spread over some 27 buildings and numbered more than 500 employees.

Leo Fender may have felt he had reached an impasse whereby more cash was needed to fuel further expansion and invest in a bigger manufacturing site. Besides, his health was worsening and he was getting increasingly tired because of a strep infection he first caught during a vacation in the mid-50s. He could no longer work as hard as he wished to or as required by the continuous development of his company. Also, his guitars and basses were tremendous hits, but he might have perceived the inception of solid state amps as a threat for his own tube design. Anyway, at some point in time, Leo Fender decided to quit and sell the devastatingly successful business he had built in less than two decades.

After a few local contacts established through the company's accountant, Don Randall – 50% owner of FENDER SALES – was allowed by Leo Fender to properly investigate the financial market in order to find a suitable buyer. Don then met with representatives from well-known Wall Street firm Merryll Lynch, who introduced him to COLUMBIA BROADCASTING SYSTEM Inc. (CBS for short) at that time in search of lucrative investments. Negotiations began in the latter part of Summer 1964 and the deal was legally closed on January 5, 1965 for a whopping $13.5m. Both FENDER ELECTRIC INSTRUMENT and FENDER SALES were acquired by CBS MUSICAL INSTRUMENTS, a division of CBS, Inc. and Fender products would then be sold as FENDER MUSICAL INSTRUMENTS.

THE CBS YEARS
1965-1984

CBS VERSUS PRE-CBS

In the eyes of most guitar buffs, the CBS take-over is considered as THE milestone in Fender's history. Numerous stories about a decline in product quality soon engendered a "pre-CBS" label meant to designate the instruments produced before Leo Fender sold out. But, what is exactly the border between a CBS and a pre-CBS instrument?

In the heart of hard-core purists, 1964 is obviously the last of the pre-CBS years. For others, the "F" stamped neck-plates which appeared in the course of 1965 are the true stigma of a CBS instrument. Conversely, L-series numbers are viewed as being pre-CBS, even though some of them were released in 1965 and sometimes early 1966. The CBS syndrome may also be analysed on a case-by-case basis, according to the modifications brought to specific models (e.g. the Stratocaster's larger peghead). Finally, it may be stated in the light of new production methods and/or the discontinuation of typical components from the Leo Fender years (e.g. Kluson tuning keys, nitro-cellulose finishes, old-style logos, "cloth wires" etc...).

Whichever one chooses, one fact remains for sure: on the threshold of the 70s, Fender instruments no longer exactly looked, felt or sometimes sounded the same as their older counterparts. Whether they were better or worse may be a matter of personal opinion, but many players agreed then they were probably not as good.

Buck Owens (right) and Don Rich (left) on stage playing silver-flake Telecaster Custom at the height of Buckaroo fever in the 60s.

'63 mabogany-bodied Telecaster and Custom model.
[courtesy Fender]

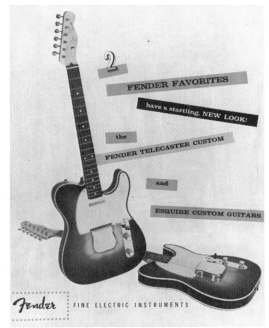
FENDER FAVORITES
have a startling NEW LOOK!
2
the
FENDER TELECASTER CUSTOM
and
ESQUIRE CUSTOM GUITARS
Fender FINE ELECTRIC INSTRUMENTS

The 1959 leaflet announcing the Custom models.
[courtesy Fender]

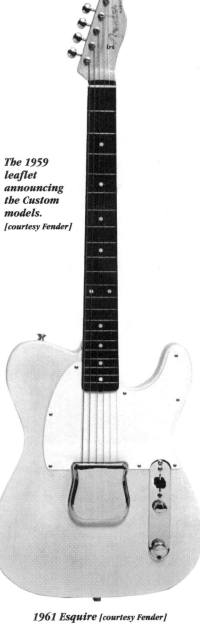

An enduring blues combination: Muddy Waters and his perennial Telecaster.

1961 Esquire [courtesy Fender]

Steve Cropper in the early days of Booker T. and the MGs.
[photo courtesy of Michael Ochs Archives]

The September 1968 "Groovy Naturals" advert introducing the lightweight Thinline model. [courtesy Fender]

Pick a winner in the Telecaster family. 1968 advert featuring a Telly with stock Bigsby tailpiece and the new Telecaster Bass. [courtesy Fender]

One of the Kenwood tractors with 40 foot long trailer used by Fender Sales in the mid-60s to move equipment between Santa Ana and Tulsa. [courtesy Fender]

James Burton with Ricky Nelson in a promo shot for Fender's late 60s "Galaxy of Stars".

Rick Nelson and James Burton play

Singer and composer Willie Nelson on stage in the late 60s. [courtesy Albert Lee]

An out-take from a mid-60s photo session for a "You won't part with yours either" advert. [courtesy Fender]

By a twist of fate, a similar syndrome struck Gibson, after Ted McCarty's departure in 1966, and Gretsch, after Baldwin's take-over in 1967. The rhetoric of "they don't make them like they used to" would soon begin to fuel a thriving "vintage market" in the 70s.

By all accounts, CBS never intended consciously to lower the quality of Fender instruments and to some extent it even attempted the opposite. After the take-over, a new 120,000 sq.ft. building with modern equipment was erected next to the existing Fullerton premises to provide a better production environment. Besides, all the key individuals who had contributed to the success of Fender products were maintained in prominent positions within the new company to ensure continuity. Leo Fender had a 5-year contract to stay as a special consultant whilst Donald Randall became president and general manager of CBS Musical Instruments. So, what went wrong?

In the wake of the take-over, CBS brought new people into the company but mostly imported a corporate bureaucracy and formal management style, probably ill-suited to the original Fender ethics. The emphasis was also firmly laid upon profits and increased productivity as later recounted by Freddie Tavares: *"We had turned into a big fancy corporation all of a sudden, where all the different departments had got their say in everything and then that was budgets, quotas and so on. They [CBS] would try to put out the stuff as fast as they could!"* (22). Production was indeed boosted by 45% during the first year of operation of the new Fullerton facility, but a decline in quality as well as new specs gradually substantiated rumours, and musicians sensed the difference between a CBS and a pre-CBS guitar. Under those circumstances, Forrest White was the first senior executive to resign, followed by Don Randall who finally left CBS in April 1969. Leo Fender terminated his 5-year contract and then quit, as did George Fullerton.

As far as Telecaster guitars are concerned, 1967 may be considered in various respects as a turning point in the CBS versus pre-CBS rhetoric. It is the year when the old 50s style circuit was deleted and replaced by a more classic wiring allowing a two-pickup combination. This point is often overlooked because many players simply clipped (in the 60s or later) the .1 MFD capacitor originally inserted by Leo between the switch and the volume pot. Also, Kluson tuners were replaced by Schaller-made Fender keys and a bigger TV-conspicuous black logo was ushered in by Fall 1967. Experiments with polyester finishes, more appropriate for mass production, would quickly lead to the discontinuation of the original, yet more unstable and polluting, nitro-cellulose lacquers.

Having said that not everything turned wrong the minute CBS took control of FENDER and the late 60s actually witnessed the introduction of several interesting Telecaster variants as well as the resurrection of "white necks." At that time, Fender's senior solid body was certainly considered as a stronger asset than the Stratocaster to complement more recent models like the Jaguar or the Jazzmaster. CBS took the view to downstream the Telecaster concept by producing additional variants meant to rejuvenate the company's original solid body electric. Incidentally, it should be noted for the record that the Telecaster trademark was filed by CBS on December 11, 1968 and registered on June 24, 1969 under No. 871,794. The registration's wording referred to an alleged introduction in the late 40s by stating "first use in or about 1949; in commerce in or about 1949."

THE CREATIVE YEARS

The shift to rosewood-capped necks in 1959 did not eradicate the wants and needs of some players for a clear maple fingerboard. Contrary to popular belief, maple-capped necks were thus produced – mostly on Telecasters – well before the option officially appeared in print in late 60s Fender brochures. The earliest example known to this author dates from 1963, but pre-63 samples may well exist. Up to 1967, though, Telecasters with a two-piece maple neck resulted from truly custom orders and were not made in great numbers. Eventually, by popular request, optional maple fingerboards were officially listed in January 1967 at an additional 5% cost. Even though this option was theoretically available on most Fender electrics, it was primarily exercised by owners of Telecaster guitars between 1967 and 1970.

By Spring 1969, the "optional maple fingerboard" ceased to be a maple cap and FENDER reverted to one-piece maple necks for Telecaster guitars. In fact, it would appear that the Maple Neck (with capital letters) first reappeared on the Telecaster Bass in 1968 prior to being offered on Telecaster guitars in early 1969 and then other Fender electrics. Incidentally, the return of the one-piece neck prompted the factory to go back to a truss-rod installation from the rear and this method was also applied – on standardisation grounds – to rosewood-capped necks. This explains why, beginning in 1969, the latter first showed a "skunk stripe" and a plug above the nut.

After 1965, Fender produced a few Custom models with a black (instead of a white) binding, mostly on guitars finished in light colour finishes such as white or yellow. In the July 1967 issue (number 14) of *Fender Facts*, a Bigsby tremolo tailpiece was first shown as an option on Telecaster guitars. The Bigsby tailpiece was made available either as a factory appointment – in which case the body was not drilled for back loading – or as a replacement kit. In both cases, the original 3-piece bridge was superseded by a Jaguar style 6-piece unit.

1967 is also the year when FENDER began experimenting in order to produce a lighter weight Telecaster. The impetus for such a lighter guitar no doubt came from commercial reasons, given both the inconsistency of the ash timber the company was procuring and the appeal of contemporary models like the Gibson SG. Anyway, the factory initially tried routing additional cavities under the pickguard, just for the sake of removing chunks of wood from the body without affecting the look of the guitar. A very small number of these "Smuggler's Tellies" were made over Summer 1967, but the attempt was not very convincing. Then came a more ambitious project called the "hollow body Telecaster" and eventually released as the TELECASTER THINLINE in mid-1968.

By all accounts, the Thinline resulted from the input of Roger Rossmeisl (R&D) and Virgilio Simoni, then head of the Blank, Body and Sanding department. It was basically a Telecaster body with pockets hollowed-out from the rear, including a bigger one opening into the top via an "f" hole. With the exception of the pickguard shape modified to accomodate the new semi-acoustic design, the Thinline was otherwise identical to a regular '68 Telecaster in terms of neck, electronics and hardware. But its body was about half the weight of a regular Telecaster.

The new variant was first listed in July 1968 for $319.50, but oddly enough it is not displayed in the 1969 catalogue, shot earlier in the previous year as was then normal practice at FENDER. To convey the idea of a lighter, almost acoustic guitar, the Thinline was at first released in only natural ash and mahogany finishes with a 2-piece maple neck, as depicted in the "groovy naturals" advert or in the November '68 issue of *Fender Facts*. By 1969, it also became available with a 3-tone sunburst finish and an optional rosewood-capped neck.

1968 also witnessed the introduction of two additional versions of the Telecaster: the PAISLEY RED and BLUE FLOWER models. Based on regular maple board Tellies, the two guitars were fitted with finishes meant to capitalize upon the emergence of Flower Power in San Francisco. The accompanying captions on the Fender leaflet were indeed worded in a contemporary spirit: "Paisley Red pulsates with every beat and swirls in a blinding carousel of color forms and tones..." and "Blue Flower bursts forth in a dazzling array of subtle purple and green patterns..." Both finishes were achieved with stickum wallpaper applied on the top and back of the body and then sprayed with polyester.

The success of the two models was not, however, as spectacular as their Paisley and Floral graphics which at the time were also available on the Telecaster Bass. Both versions were discontinued in late 1969 when the San Francisco sound gave way to the early flurries of metal rock à la Led Zeppelin. Rather than a perfect match for the late 60s Haight-Ashbury scene, the Paisley Red Telecaster would later go down in history as a trademark guitar for James BURTON. The last samples (like the one used by James) were produced with a one-piece maple neck instead of a separate maple fretboard.

James Burton with his 1969 Paisley Telecaster backing Emmylou Harris in the mid-70s.
[courtesy Warner Bros]

1968 maple board Telecaster with floral (left) and paisley (above) stickum graphics.
[courtesy Fender]

One-off Telecaster in zebrawood with one-piece rosewood neck.
[photo by John Sprung]

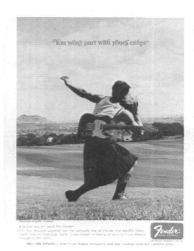

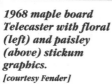

1966-67 "You won't part with yours either" advert.

Early 1969 Thinline with sunburst finish.
[courtesy Pete Alenov]

George Harrison with his Rosewood Telecaster during the Beatles' "Let It Be" sessions. [courtesy Apple Corps Ltd]

· The third innovative design to come out in the CBS early years was the ROSEWOOD TELECASTER, initially designed as a special guitar for George HARRISON. Back in the 60s, there is no denying that the sales of Gretsch and Rickenbacker guitars (and to a lesser extent Gibson and Epiphone) were substantially boosted during the peak period of Beatlemania. However, Fender instruments were not featured with the BEATLES until George gave some exposure to the Stratocaster in the Magical Mystery Tour TV film released in December 1967. Probably in a gesture of appreciation, FENDER presented George HARRISON with a custom-made solid Rosewood Telecaster in 1968. The instrument can be heard on the *Let It Be* sessions (*Get Back!*) and George also used it for the Apple "roof concert" in January 1969 before giving it later to Delaney Bramlett.

In early 1969 the Rosewood model was added to the Fender line and became at $375 the most expensive Telecaster then ever listed. The electronics were identical to a regular Telly and, apart from an all-rosewood construction, the only modification was a triple ply black guard. The very first samples were built with a (heavy!) solid rosewood body, but FENDER quickly changed for two lighter hollowed-out body halves sandwiching a thin maple strip. Unlike George's two-piece neck, production guitars were fitted with a one-piece rosewood neck, similar in construction to the original Maple Neck. Owing to both the cost of rosewood and its peculiar mode of construction, the model was not produced in quantity. As a matter of fact, the Rosewood Telecaster was not permanently listed between 1969 and 1972 and, for instance, its production was temporarily suspended after mid-1970. At any rate, the model would be definitely discontinued after mid-1972.

In 1969, the Telecaster range counted no less than six basic variants, not to mention the Paisley/Floral patterns, the optional custom finishes and Bigsby tailpiece or the choice of a rosewood/maple cap for the neck. In short, it was then the most prolific guitar in the Fender line while being its most enduring design. Late 60s catalogues stressed "This is the guitar that starts it all. Rhythm and Blues and Country too are played better on the Telecaster than on any other guitar in the world" or "...a lead tone that can't be equalled."

Since the mid-60s, the Telecaster had gained new exponents in all sorts of music styles. In the early days of the Who, Pete TOWNSHEND bruised a couple of Tellies playing maximum R&B whilst Ray DAVIES really got it with the Kinks. Mike BLOOMFIELD not only became a respected bluesman but he also set trends by putting a humbucker in the neck position of his Telecaster. During his 1965-66 world tour Bob DYLAN fronted the HAWKS with a Telly whilst singers like Willie NELSON or Waylon JENNINGS were also playing one on their path to fame. With the Yardbirds, Jeff BECK and Jimmy PAGE were planting the seeds of heavy rock respectively using an Esquire and a Telecaster. Whether for lead or rhythm playing, the Telecaster was still a clear favourite 20 years after it had been designed.

On the threshold of the 70s, FENDER too was bigger than ever with a personnel close to 950 employees and combined facilities exceeding 300,000 sq.ft. in the Fullerton area. After the take-over CBS invested some $2.7m in a modern building adjacent to the former Fender premises to enlarge substantially the production capacity. At first the sales department of FENDER MUSICAL INSTRUMENTS remained headquartered in Santa Ana, where it had all started with RTEC and FENDER SALES. Once Don Randall left the company in Spring 1969, the huge 175,000 sq.ft. building erected on Valencia Avenue became FENDER's sole headquarters to the detriment of the old East Chestnut address in Santa Ana. Times were a-changin'...

A WIND OF CHANGE

The 70s are often considered as the darker period in the CBS era, i.e. one during which Fender instruments lost some of the the quality and features which had so far contributed to their reputation. Many changes effectively took place during the 70s and not always for the better, as later acknowledged by the company itself!

The earliest changes were actually deletions, such as the discontinuation of the single pickup ESQUIRE in late 1969. What FENDER termed an "economically priced modern instrument" in the 50s gradually appeared redundant during the 60s as the model sold indeed in fewer and fewer numbers. Besides, the initial rationale to skim the market could no longer apply with guitars like the Mustang retailing for less than a regular Esquire.

The next models to be dropped from the catalogue in 1972 were the ROSEWOOD TELECASTER and the CUSTOM model with a bound body. Again, straight economics played their part in the decision as the Rosewood Telly was too expensive to produce whilst the Custom was not such a good seller. At that time, FENDER was keen to promote the original Telecaster model with a Blond finish as illustrated by the (in)famous advert: "The 1948 Telecaster – The 1972 Telecaster: You're looking at identical twins." Incidentally, in 1976, another advert entitled "the high-flying mellow-throated Telecaster" – depicting the instrument in the guise of an eagle – even mentioned that it was "first sighted soaring to unheard-of altitudes in 1946" (!). Anyway, the last Customs with white binding were made in Spring 1972, just before Fender retrieved the name to introduce a totally different instrument under the same designation.

The early 70s equally saw a drastic reduction in the palette of custom colours and ultimately the disappearance of the very notion of "custom finish." By 1975 only Black, White, Natural and Walnut were listed as "standard" finishes in addition to Blond and Sunburst. Gone were the automotive paints borrowed from G.M. or Ford, but this was not just CBS's fault. Natural-looking finishes were the new craze, not solid colours, and many players were even sanding off the body of their guitar to remove all colour paint. Both Natural and Walnut finishes were thus introduced by FENDER in 1972 to capitalize upon this new popular trend, whilst classic colours like Lake Placid Blue or Candy Apple Red were deleted.

Beyond aesthetics – which are after all a matter of personal taste – Fender also developed (and trademarked) its "thick-skin high-gloss finish." Polyester is probably better suited to industrial mass-production and more stable than nitro-cellulose, but heavier coats of polyester contributed to the rather "plasticky" looks of 70s Fender instruments. Lacquer finishes and their gently weathered looks with ageing belonged to the past.

However, the final straw, i.e. the most disparaged feature to appear on Fender electrics during the CBS years, was for many the "Tilt Neck." While he stayed as a consultant for CBS Musical Instruments, Leo Fender came up with what he called a "tiltable guitar neck incorporating thrust-absorbing pivot and locking element." The purpose of this device was to facilitate neck pitch adjustment via a small Allen screw located in the anchor plate, instead of inserting little shims in the neck pocket. Simultaneously, the truss-rod adjusting bolt was removed from the neck heel and housed in a bullet above the nut. The concept was attractive for players but its materialization entailed a 3-bolt neck mounting in lieu of the classic 4-bolt. This feature engendered suspicion of a less efficient neck joint and contributed to fuelling unfavourable comments about CBS instruments. The patent for the Tilt Neck was granted to Leo Fender on December 29, 1970 and by 1971 the first Fender electrics were equipped with the new device. Contrary to what the patent drawing might suggest, the regular Telecaster was not among the chosen few, but the other variants available during the rest of the 70s were all fitted with a Tilt Neck.

The 60s blues boom and the ensuing transition towards heavy rock gave exposure to Gibson-type double coil humbuckers because of their sustain and weeping tone. As FENDER later claimed in a 1972 leaflet: "Humbucking pickups eliminate feedback and add a gutty mid-range and bass sound." In the late 60s, however, the Fender sound was mostly associated with bright sounding single coil units and CBS MUSICAL INSTRUMENTS felt the commercial need to enlarge its pickup offering. Meanwhile, Seth LOVER, the man who had designed Gibson's famous humbucker in the mid-50s, resigned from his job in Kalamazoo in 1967. When Dick Evans, a former Gibson employee then working in Fullerton, heard of Seth's resignation he invited him to California. Guess what happened: Seth Lover was hired by FENDER and he subsequently designed the company's first double coil pickup (available in a guitar and bass version).

Compared to a classic late 60s humbucker, the new Fender unit was primarily characterized by twelve adjustable cunife magnets and a mega output (DC resistance > 10k Ohms). Seth Lover's new humbucking pickup was finalized in the course of 1970 and first appeared on Fender instruments after mid-1971. Telecaster guitars were initially the sole recipient of the newly designed pickup, also fitted later to the short-lived Starcaster. By the end of 1971, the THINLINE was thus revamped with two humbuckers and a Tilt Neck. The second variant of the semi-acoustic model, first listed in February 1972, otherwise incorporated a modified pickguard, a 6-piece Strat-style bridge and a "Thinline" decal on the upper bout of the headstock. At first it retained the same basic finishes as the original Thinline, i.e. Ash, Mahogany and Sunburst, but very few were actually made in mahogany before this finish was dropped.

In mid-1972, FENDER came up with a more extensive redesign and introduced a new version of the TELECASTER CUSTOM equipped with one humbucker in the neck position. Even though it retained the Custom name, the guitar was indeed a totally new instrument having little in common with its forerunner apart from the overall shape and the single coil bridge pickup, hence a change in its product number from 11-1400 to 11-0700. By and large, the Custom type II was intended as a hybrid combining the best of both worlds. Earlier on, players like Mike BLOOMFIELD or Albert LEE had already stuck a humbucking pickup in the forward position of their Telecaster and FENDER simply standardized the process with the new 1972 Custom. Otherwise, the guitar was fitted with a Tilt Neck and sported an elongated black pickguard with 4 controls and a 3-way toggle switch. The earliest production models were released with the original Telecaster bridge, but an upgraded 6-piece design was soon installed for an improved intonation.

To foster FENDER's quest for a new clientele, a third variant with humbuckers made its debut in January 1973 as the TELECASTER DELUXE. Marketed then as the higher grade model in the Telecaster family, the Deluxe was in many respects a composite design blending appointments from other Fender guitars. It thus featured a Strat-style Tilt Neck (with a larger peghead) and 6-piece bridge, also available with optional tremolo action (discontinued after 1974). The guitar retained the overall Telecaster shape but the back of the body was contoured à la Stratocaster. Electronically, it sported two humbuckers like the revamped Thinline, mounted on a black pickguard assembly similar to the Custom, with four controls and a 3-way toggle switch. In short, the TELECASTER DELUXE was basically a "Stratocasterized Telly with humbuckers." Like the Thinline II it was exclusively available with a Maple Neck, whilst the Custom could be ordered with either a rosewood board or or Maple Neck.

The three Telecasters with humbuckers probably brought a new breed of customers to Fender during the 70s but they somehow failed to attract the traditional Gibson clientele, particularly at a time when the Les Paul mystique was gathering momentum. Besides, with the possible exception of the "hybrid" Custom, they equally failed to impress hard core Telly players. Rolling Stone Keith RICHARDS did add the Custom to his favourite instruments but he also remained faithful to his '54 Telecaster retrofitted with a Gibson humbucker. So did Terry KATH guitarist with Chicago and Andy SUMMERS, later of Police fame. The Thinline was eventually dropped in 1979 whilst the Deluxe and Custom models were discontinued in early 1981.

During the 70s, besides the very specs of its guitars, the pre-CBS notion took root as FENDER priced itself out of the market and produced lower quality instruments. Over the decade the economy obviously suffered from the impact of the oil crisis and inflationary trends, but CBS's high margin policy brought about hefty raises in list price. Whilst a regular Telecaster with rosewood board listed for $283 in 1973, it spiralled to $635 (+224%!) by 1980.

Thanks to a rather weak dollar in foreign terms, the demand from export markets was brisk and Fullerton was churning out lots of instruments. But their quality was going downhill because of a lack of appropriate control and

investment in the manufacturing facility. For instance, the decision was made to only use one type of wood (ash) for solid bodies, but the purchasing department omitted to stipulate weight as a prime consideration. As a result, the guitars from this period are on the whole the heaviest ever produced. The installation of modern equipment for added productivity also impacted the actual design of some models. Regarding Telecaster guitars, the inception of numerically-controlled routers brought about subtle, yet graceless, changes in the body shape. At the end of the day, the 70s instruments largely contributed to the craze for pre-CBS "vintage" models.

Despite these inconveniences, the all-purpose Telecaster was still in the spotlight as a common denominator among artists as diverse as Roy BUCHANAN, Ted GREENE, STATUS QUO, Bruce SPRINGSTEEN, the CLASH's Joe STRUMMER or the OSMOND BROTHERS just to name a few! On the threshold of the 80s, however, a loss in market share against competitors, not to mention stagnating profits, prompted CBS to recruit a new top management in order to upgrade FENDER and put it more in tune with what was happening in the music industry.

CBS SWAN SONG

In early 1981 John McLaren and Bill Schultz, formerly with Yamaha, became respectively president of the CBS MUSICAL INSTRUMENTS division and FENDER, with Roger Balmer as VP in charge of sales and marketing. Initial appraisals outlined several nagging issues which needed to be promptly addressed. An internal report from May 1981 thus cited "a significant increase in domestic and foreign dealer complaints about defective and unacceptable quality" or "a policy of high margins and little product improvement." In a memo to Bill Schultz, Chuck Van Liew, director of manufacturing, indicated that "with the exception of 1977, Fullerton has been on a program of restricted capital investment" and proceeded to itemize a $2.5m list of machines needed to upgrade the production facility.

CBS had made a lot of money with FENDER in the 70s, but little had been invested back into the company. Over the 1971/1980 period the annual sales of FENDER/ROGERS/RHODES grew from $18.8m to $60.5m but, while pre-tax profit averaged more than $9m p.a., capital expenditures barely reached $0.75m p.a. and R&D a mere $0.6m p.a. (i.e. less than 1.4% of net sales over the period). It was time for CBS to spare some capital for its musical division, and plans were immediately devised by the new management team to restore Fender's competitive position. In this connection, Dan Smith was in turn called from Yamaha to become director of marketing for electric guitars and basses.

Meanwhile, the annual Summer trade show was drawing near and new models had to be shown to keep FENDER on the move, whilst the 70s Deluxe and Custom were being discontinued. Prior to the management reshuffle, the company had finally realized that well-known players were usually keener on older pre-CBS models than on more recent guitars. In 1980, it was therefore decided to recreate a classic Telecaster and the development of a '52 reissue began under Freddie Tavares' supervision. At the June 1981 NAMM show in Chicago, the VINTAGE TELECASTER was thus introduced as a limited edition model whose production (3000 guitars) was scheduled to start in August. However, if Freddie Tavares took trouble to research the original 1952 specs, the prototype exhibited at the show was built with the factory regular jigs and fixtures, hence a wrong body shape (and a wrong mustard finish!). When Dan Smith came on board in August 1981, he immediately suspended production of the new Telecaster.

The other variant to appear at the June 1981 show was the BLACK & GOLD TELECASTER. Offered with either a Maple Neck or a rosewood fretboard, the B&G was basically a regular Telly finished in black (including a painted-on headcap) and fitted with gold-plate brass hardware. Its massive 6-piece bridge was designed with a heavy ridge for additional sustain in line with contemporary popular trends. Actually, the B&G was pretty much a "Schecterized Telecaster" built around the brass works accessories launched by FENDER the previous year in order to seize a share in the then buoyant market of retrofitting hardware. Unlike the Vintage reissue, it went into production by Summer 1981 and thus kept for almost nine months the 70s wrong body shape.

The 1970s revamped Telecaster Custom
[courtesy Fender]

1972 advert...
"You're looking at
identical twins!"

Keith Richards playing an early 50s
Telecaster retrofitted with a humbucker
in the neck position.

The 1948 Telecaster.   The 1972 Telecaster.

Two generations of Thinline: the
original issue (bottom) and the
type II with humbuckers (top).
[courtesy Buck Sulcer]

lbert Lee in the
rly 70s playing
a rosewood
board Telly
uring his stint
with Heads
Hands and Feet.
ourtesy Yves Farge]

1974 dragster advert..."You get there faster
on a Fender!"

1970s Deluxe in non-tremolo version
[courtesy Fender]

The late Roy Buchanan pictured in 1982 at the Lone Star club in New York city.
[photo by John Peden]

1983 Walnut Elite

1983 Standard Telecaster

The 1981 Vintage Reissue as finally introduced with a correct body shape.
[courtesy Fender]

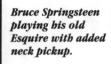

Bruce Springsteen playing his old Esquire with added neck pickup.

Jazz guitarist and long time Telly connoisseur Ted Greene tries out the Vintage Reissue at the January 1982 NAMM show.
[courtesy Dan Smith]

When Dan Smith became director of marketing in August 1981, he was asked to produce quickly a 5-year plan in order to revive sales, develop new products and also restore the dented image of Fender. In early September, the plan was okayed by Thomas Wyman, then chairman and CEO of CBS Inc. and the first steps were taken to upgrade the Fullerton facility. As recalled by Dan: *"Basically our goal was initially to restore the confidence of the dealers and the players in Fender. The only way we could achieve that was to raise the quality levels back up! [...] We basically shut the plant down and retaught everybody how to make Fender guitars the way people wanted them"* (23). By Fall, production fell from around 250/300 guitars per day down to just a handful to permit a complete rethink of the manufacturing process.

Product-wise, the first projects to materialise were the Vintage Reissues and a lifting of regular production models. In the latter part of 1981, Dan Smith and R&D senior engineer John Page carried out extensive research to come up with modern replicas of several old-style guitars and basses. The whole series featuring a '57 and '62 Stratocaster, a '57 and '62 Precision Bass, a '62 Jazz Bass and...a '52 Telecaster was unveiled in January 1982 at the Winter NAMM show in Anaheim, but actual production did not start until much later in the year. By then, the VINTAGE TELECASTER had a correct body shape, and it was no longer a limited edition but a full-flight production guitar delivered with a certificate of authenticity (and a kit of modern retrofitting parts). Incidentally, the inception of a classic Telly design brought about the discontinuation of Blond finish on the other variants.

Simultaneously, a refined STANDARD TELECASTER with the right body shape was made available with six standard and seven custom finishes. To herald clearly the change in attitude towards the market, Dan Smith also came up with what is probably the most lavish catalogue ever published by FENDER, with prominent pictures of famed Telly players like James BURTON, Steve CROPPER, Albert LEE, Roy BUCHANAN and Ted GREENE.

The next project was the Elite series whose development was also initiated in the latter part of 1981 and took some 18 months to come to fruition. The Elite concept was an ambitious attempt to blend tradition with modern technologies, and as such its focal points were upgraded electronics, better neck adjustment and more functional hardware. Overall, the goal was to produce more flexible instruments with a contemporary look and feel. As far as the ELITE TELECASTER is concerned, the idea was once more to entice Gibson players, as readily admitted by Dan Smith: *"The attempt was also to pick up some of the Gibson players, hence the Les Paul-type switch and the humbucking pickups"* (24).

The Elite Telecaster was thus designed as a "balls-out" loud guitar fitted with two humbuckers, four controls, a 3-way toggle switch and a white binding on the top edge of the body. Otherwise, it featured the novel appointments common to the Elite series like a Biflex truss-rod, a flatter fretboard radius (12") with jumbo fretwire, a heavy duty cast bridge with drop-in string loading and of course active electronics with a special tone circuitry (MDX and TBX controls). Three versions were simultaneously introduced at the June 1983 NAMM show: the ELITE TELECASTER with chrome-plated hardware, the GOLD ELITE TELECASTER with gold-plated hardware and pearloid-button tuners and the WALNUT ELITE TELECASTER crafted in American black walnut (body and neck) with an ebony fretboard, gold-plated hardware and pearloid-button tuners. A tremolo version and a 22-fret neck were also on the drawing board, but CBS's decision in mid-1984 to divest from Fender prevented these additional appointments from hitting the production line.

In many respects, the Elite series did outline the renewed creative capacity of FENDER, but in an otherwise fairly conservative guitar world, it did not prove a milestone as anticipated by its originators.

The Elite models signalled the end of the Black & Gold Telecaster, but FENDER also announced a revised STANDARD TELECASTER with a Biflex truss-rod and a flatter 12" fretboard radius. Compared to previous versions, though, its most salient features were a new top-loaded bridge assembly with six elongated Elite saddles (and no cover) and the absence of copper plate at the bottom of the lead pickup.

The combination of all these ingredients resulted in a different kind of Telecaster, with more mid-range but not really the sound and feel of a normal Telly.

Beyond these specific appointments, FENDER's main objective was to produce a reasonably-priced Telecaster and indeed, at $550 with case, the guitar was significantly less expensive than the previous standard model which listed for $820 in January 1983. The choice of finishes was restricted to four basic colours, but in late 1984 a special run of 75 guitars was made with colourful marble finishes (a.k.a. "bowling ball" finishes) in red, gold and blue (25 samples each) and sold with assorted matching T-shirts.

To complete a totally revised product offering, a fourth project was also conceived by Dan Smith but never materialized production-wise: the ULTRA TELECASTER. Intended as the ultimate top-model, the guitar would have featured a neck-through-body construction, an ebony fretboard with snowflake inlays, two humbucking pickups and a tremolo. Only two prototypes were built, one in koa wood and one with a walnut/maple lamination, but constraints in production capacity plus the CBS decision to get rid of FENDER shelved the whole project (but the name would resurface a few years later with the Ultra Stratocaster).

The final leg of the strategy drafted in 1981 was the establishment of "offshore" production to counter the explosion in copies and clones of Fender guitars made in Japan (or elsewhere!). Affordable budget guitars were needed to recapture the lower end of the market, but the environment then prevailing in the USA was not appropriate for such a project. In December 1981, FENDER entered into negotiations with Japanese companies KANDA SHOKAI Corp. and YAMANO MUSIC Co. for the creation of FENDER JAPAN Co. Ltd. The American-Japanese joint venture was established in March 1982 and Fender-branded guitars were henceforth manufactured in Japan by FUJI GEN-GAKKI Mfg Co., Ltd.

Those "made in Japan" instruments were intended for the local domestic market but also exported to Europe where they caused some confusion among dealers and players. In late 1982, the Squier brand name, which belonged to FENDER MUSICAL INSTRUMENTS since 1965, was therefore activated (initially with a "Squire" spelling) on the instruments distributed outside Japan. At this stage, Japanese models were aimed at protecting FENDER's share in overseas markets but none of them was then meant for sale in the USA. However, the stronger value of the dollar prompted the US management to acknowledge that it also needed agressively priced items to be competitive on its home market. As later recalled by Dan Smith: *"Finally in 1983, we felt that we had to bring these guitars into the USA to be able to compete with other people that were taking our business. We tried everything we could to see if we could produce guitars in the US for below $500 and this was just not possible!"* (25). By late 1983, a Squier Telecaster became available in the USA where it listed for $369 (less case) compared to $589 for its American counterpart.

This offshore strategy may be open to criticism in the eyes of those who believe that a genuine Fender guitar has to be made in California, or at least in the USA. Beyond any emotional issue, Japanese instruments eventually helped FENDER once CBS proceeded to pull out the plug. Despite a spate of improvements since 1981, FENDER was having difficulty in showing a turnaround in profits. After citing "red ink" in its Musical Instruments division as part of its poor interim results in 1984, CBS informed Bill Schultz in July 1984 that Fender would be put up for sale on the open market.

A few serious corporate buyers such as KAMAN Corp. or I.M.C. were the first to bid for the company, but in November 1964 CBS accepted the principle of a management buy-out led by Bill Schultz. After weeks of rumours and speculation, a statement released on the opening day of the 1985 Winter NAMM show marked the end of an era. CBS announced that: "It has agreed in principle to sell Fender Musical Instruments, a unit of CBS Inc. to an investor group led by William Schultz, president of Fender Musical Instruments, for an undisclosed price. A definite agreement is currently being finalized and a signing is expected shortly." Both parties entered into a contract on February 8, 1985 and the sale was legally completed on March 12, 1985. After two decades of pre-CBS semantics, the post-CBS nomenclature was open!

A NEW ERA
1985-1991 (PRESENT)

BACK TO BASICS

The huge Fullerton facility was not included in the agreement with CBS, as explained by Dan Smith: *"Because of the nature of the business at that time and the amount of money that we could raise, we didn't buy the land and the buildings that CBS also owned. The Fullerton building [...] was a very large plant and it was beyond the size of what we needed for how we planned to do business"* (26). But, in early 1985 Bill Schultz also mentioned that: *"Contrary to some rumours, Fender products will continue to be made in the US, as well as in other countries"* (27). The questions then were which products and which production site in the US ?

When CBS proceeded to sell FENDER in 1984, the personnel was rapidly brought down from 700 people to about 200 and later to a "workable number" of 110 when the Fullerton factory effectively closed down in early 1985. The suspension of manufacturing activities triggered slashed prices on the inventory of US made guitars (e.g. $699 for a Gold Elite as opposed to $1059 a year before) as well as a massive inclusion of Japanese instruments in the current catalogue. By June, the headquarters of the newly-independent FENDER MUSICAL INSTRUMENTS Corp. were relocated in nearby Brea, on 1130 Columbia(!) street. Over Summer, after considering various locations in Southern California, suitable production premises were found in the city of Corona, off the Riverside freeway. At the end of October 1985 FENDER was again in a position to build American-made guitars, albeit in more limited quantities.

In 1985, the dollar reached unprecedented peaks against other currencies and this simply meant that US made guitars were moderately competitive on export markets. The plan was therefore to scale down the local operation and rely more on offshore production. Owing to their popularity, the Vintage Reissues – more specifically the '57 and '62 Stratocasters – were the first guitars built in Corona. But, with only 10 people on the floor, the initial output was limited to a mere 5 guitars per day compared to about 200 before the CBS spin-off. Despite an obvious emphasis on Stratocasters, the VINTAGE TELECASTER was again listed as early as January 1986. It was at first produced in small numbers, partly because of a limited production capacity, partly because Fender was having difficulties in procuring light-weight "punk ash."

The next US Telecaster to be listed was the AMERICAN STANDARD, officially introduced at the January 1988 Winter NAMM Convention in Anaheim. Designed by George Blanda, senior R&D engineer, the new variant was actually pencilled in the wake of its Stratocaster namesake, but its production was delayed until late 1987 because of constraints in Corona. Thanks to more favourable exchange rates (i.e. a declining dollar), FENDER found itself in a situation whereby it could enlarge its range of US made guitars, hence the choice of a meaningful designation vis-à-vis the Japanese made instruments also marketed by the company.

Compared to the 1983-85 variant, the newer Standard incorporates a few changes such as a 9.5" fretboard radius, a 22-fret neck, a revised bridge assembly with compressed steel saddles and a TBX tone control. It also features an alder body and a neck with a matter satin finish. However, like the previous standard model, the lead pickup has been left without a copper back plate to produce a sound with more mid-range than the '52 reissue.

With a fast-rising production to meet demand for its US models, FENDER steadily hired extra personnel (often former CBS employees) and leased additional space in the Corona industrial complex. By early 1987, production topped 100 guitars per day and looked set to increase at a brisk pace. To meet numerous players' request, FENDER also created in early 1987 a CUSTOM DESIGN GUITAR & MANUFACTURING facility, headed by Michael Stevens, well-known craftsman from Austin, Texas and John Page, former senior engineer in the R&D department. Established in Corona, albeit in specific premises adjacent to the factory, the

Custom Shop's original brief was to build one-off superlative Fender guitars as well as to produce customized parts for standard models (e.g. special necks, bodies, finishes etc...). The new operation proved an instant success and its scope was soon extended to the production of small runs of limited editions and custom-ordered instruments. Accordingly, other luthiers like Jay Black, Fred Stuart, Larry Brooks or Yasuhiko Iwanade as well as several apprentices gradually joined forces with Mike and John to meet a heavier workload.

Tele-wise, the first project engineered by the Custom Shop was the 40TH ANNIVERSARY TELECASTER introduced in June 1988. Prompted by the notion that the Telecaster first appeared in 1948 as the Broadcaster, it was meant as a commemorative model with unique appointments. Globally based on the American Standard design, the 40th Anniversary is characterized by a bound ash body with bookmatched flame maple top, a curly Maple Neck with abalone inlays, pearloid button tuners, a grained ivoroid pickguard and gold-plated parts. However, owing to plating problems, the bridge saddles actually kept a stainless steel appearance, which otherwise conveys a Rolex look to the whole assembly.

The 40th Anniversary was released in only three finishes: Antique 2-tone sunburst, Natural and see-through red, each showcasing the striking maple top. It was truly a limited edition and only 300 were painstakingly produced between Summer 1988 and early 1990 with a distinctive serial number (X of 300) and a special certificate.

THE SIGNATURE MODELS

Naming a model after a well-known artist – whether or not he has contributed to its design – was not a fresh idea and many manufacturers had already done so in the past, with the notable exception of FENDER. Today, for the record, the Eric Clapton Stratocaster is the first Signature model ever produced by FENDER, but it was not exactly the company's first attempt to build a "namesake guitar." Actually, the earliest Signature model could well have been the James Burton as such a project was first discussed with James in mid-81 while he was invited to the Fullerton factory for the launch of the '52 reissue!

The rationale behind the Fender Signature models is to build a guitar identical to the instrument actually played by an artist, as explained by Dan Smith: *"Our desire with the whole Signature Series was to build the guitars exactly the way the artists play them. We didn't just want to build something that everybody was going to buy and then the artist had to have his different"* (28). For practical purposes, this rationale would generate two types of Signature models: either dead copies of the instrument already played by the artist or a new improved design meant to encompass his ultimate needs.

When James Burton resumed talks with FENDER, he took the second route as he wanted a Telecaster with a broader tone spectrum. To this end, James requested a third pickup in the middle position for Strat-style sound variations. In terms of electronics, he became interested in the radically new Fender-Lace sensors which first appeared on the Strat Plus in 1987. At first, only the 50s-type gold sensor was available but other variants (silver, blue, red) were soon devised to cater for a variety of sounds. After a period of trials and errors, J.B. finally settled for three different Lace sensors as he discovered the distinct tones he liked in each version. A 5-way switch was then added with a specific wiring to provide appropriate combinations.

Structurally, the guitar is built around a light ash body and an ovalled-shape satin finish Maple Neck with a 9.5" fretboard radius. James kept the original 21-fret neck with a traditional truss-rod instead of the more recent 22-fret neck with Biflex. Several options were considered for the finish but since 1969 a Paisley Red Telecaster was pretty much James' trademark instrument. A modern rendition of the original Paisley graphic was also designed as an optional appointment. Unlike the late 60s stickum feature, the new Paisley finish is silkscreened for a more durable finish.

James worked back and forth with FENDER R&D (in particular George Blanda) to finalize his Signature model. The earliest prototypes were completed in late 1988, but the JAMES BURTON TELECASTER was not officially announced

until January 1990 at the Winter NAMM show where it was released in four distinct finishes:

- black with Gold Paisley and gold-plated hardware
- black with Candy Red Paisley and black chromed hardware
- Pearl White with gold hardware and no Paisley graphics
- Frost Red with black hardware and no Paisley graphics

Incidentally, the Candy Red Paisley finish is achieved by spraying transparent red over a black guitar with a silkscreened Gold Paisley. Anyway, more than 8 years after he was first talked into it, James Burton signed a contract with FENDER on November 22, 1989 to finally lend his name to a Telecaster!

Meanwhile, three other Signature models were also initiated with patented Telly players. The first one was the ALBERT COLLINS TELECASTER which is a faithful replica of the 1966 Custom exclusively used (with a Dm6 open tuning) by the legendary bluesman. Custom Shop luthier Larry Brooks built the prototype after carefully checking Albert's original instrument down to the most subtle details.

Introduced in June 1990, the Collins basically features a natural ash body with a white binding mounted with a 2-piece maple neck sporting a gold transition Fender logo. The neck specifications and measurements (width or thickness) have been accurately reproduced as well as the hardware. More specifically, the guitar is characterized by a Gibson-type humbucker in the neck position, a 70s style 6-way bridge and a glittery plastic adhesive (a.k.a. "Mexican chrome") on the snap-on bridge cover. Unlike the Burton Signature model, however, it is not meant as a regular production item but built on a custom-order basis only (hence a hefty $2400 price tag!).

The next Signature project involved master bender JERRY DONAHUE, whose model has yet to be officially introduced at the time of going to print. Jerry, like James Burton, has chosen to develop a new design incorporating a specific wiring circuit whose specifications are not yet entirely finalized.

Structurally, the proto built so far features a one-piece curly Maple Neck (with a slight "V" feel) mounted on a bound ash body with a maple top and back. It is finished in a dark 2-tone sunburst and fitted with a black pickguard and gold-plated hardware. Besides its unique wiring circuit, J.D.'s guitar is also equipped with a Stratocaster pickup in the neck position, but slightly closer than usual to the bridge unit. According to FENDER, as soon as the electronic circuit currently tested is okayed, the Donahue will be added to the Signature series as a custom-order model.

Chronologically, the third model to hit the drawing board was the DANNY GATTON TELECASTER, which made its debut alongside the Albert Collins model in mid-1990. In the same vein as Albert's guitar, the Gatton is a replica of the customized '53 Telly used until recently by the multi-style virtuoso from Washington, DC.

The D.G.'s Signature model is equipped with special double blade humbuckers, made by Joe Barden, which fit in the same space as Fender single coil pickups. These side-by-side humbucking pickups are not built for an extra gain but aim at reproducing a high fidelity version of the 50s Fender sound. In addition to the actual specs and measurements of the original instrument, Custom Shop master luthier Michael Stevens made sure to replicate the peculiar ergonomic features of Danny's '53 such as zirconium side dots (to see and feel the neck under dimmed lights), angled stainless steel saddles, a notched bridge side-plate and a bent switch lever.

The back of the neck has no finish so as not to impede playing speed, whilst the body is painted in a light Blond colour, half butterscotch-half Mary Kaye. Compared to his original '53 Telecaster, the sole modification requested by Danny was a 22-fret neck for a slightly extended treble register. Like the Collins, the Gatton Telecaster is available only on a custom-order basis and warrants the same price tag. Having said that, Michael Stevens and FENDER certainly did a good job because after he received his Signature guitar Danny simply traded his old '53 for a 1934 Ford Sedan! Since then, however, he has again personalized his own guitar, now finished in a deep gold colour enhanced by a delicate white pattern.

Besides the "official" Signature models, the Custom Shop has built several Telecasters to special order for well known artists such as Waylon Jennings (a replica of his old Custom) or Robben Ford (a wider-bodied version with a curly top and three pickups). Small runs of various old-style Tellies like the Rosewood or the Thinline type I have also been produced. All these instruments can be identified by a small Custom Shop gold decal, usually applied on the back of the headstock.

THE LATEST TELECASTERS

The success of the Strat Plus introduced in 1987 led FENDER to consider a Telecaster counterpart, i.e. a Tele Plus with Lace sensors. However, as pointed out by Dan Smith: *"The Tele Plus was made in response to the demand for Lace sensors, but we wanted to capture more of a market than just Telly players!"* (29). Development began under the supervision of George Blanda in late 1988, but the new variant did not make its debut until June 1990. During this period, various Lace sensors combinations were tried to produce a guitar offering different Telecaster sounds. The research carried out at the same time on the Burton Telecaster and the Ultra Strat eventually helped define the model's final specifications.

The TELE PLUS is equipped with a blue sensor in the neck position and a dual red in the bridge position. Unlike the early prototypes, the production guitars have a mini switch between the volume and tone controls to split the dual red sensor (i.e. two red sensors hooked up in series or individually) and provide additional combinations. The model is available in two versions: the Plus standard and the Plus Deluxe, fitted with a Strat-style tremolo, a Wilkinson Roller Nut and Schaller keys with string-locking mechanism. Otherwise, both versions feature a combined ash/alder body and a 22-fret neck with either a one-piece maple neck or a rosewood board.

As hinted at in the previous paragraphs, a strong emulation has always existed since the 50s between FENDER and its arch-rival GIBSON to be the leading American brand in the field of solid-body electrics. Over the past decades, FENDER tried different appointments and features to attract Gibson players, while sticking to its traditional bolted-neck construction. In fact, the one thing the company did not attempt was to build a guitar with a Gibson-style glued-on neck simply because its production methods and workforce were not geared to it. The advent of the Custom Shop and the recruitment of experienced luthiers gave FENDER the technical ability to build any type of guitar. Still, the question was how to produce in fair quantities a glued-on neck model without an extensive retooling or retraining?

In Spring 1990 John Page, recently appointed manager of the R&D department and the Custom Shop operations, and Steve Boulanger, Custom Shop engineer, developed a novel type of neck joint to solve this predicament. From this moment on, it became indeed possible for FENDER to produce a "set-neck" guitar without a classic dovetail joint or a finely balanced neck pitch. The new neck joint – in the process of being patented – was immediately applied on a new breed of Telecaster guitars. With the help of Jay Black, two prototypes were quickly put together for the June 1990 NAMM Convention to test the waters with dealers. In a matter of weeks, orders began to pour in and on July 26, 1990 the SET NECK TELECASTER was officially included in the Fender price list.

The Set Neck could be termed as a classic blend between a Fender and a Gibson solid body. The mahogany body is enhanced by a bookmatched curly maple top with a contrasting white binding, but to make the guitar lighter than, say a Les Paul, and improve its resonance, the core body is drilled with eleven 1.5" dia. cavities. The neck is also made of mahogany, reinforced with a maple insert for extra rigidity whilst the headstock is painted-on to add a touch of class. The 22-fret board has a flat 12" radius and, depending upon the version, is made of either Brazilian rosewood or ebony. Three distinct versions of the Set Neck Telecaster have been simultaneously introduced over Summer 1990:

- the basic model has two DiMarzio humbuckers, a rosewood fretboard and no tremolo;

The prototype of the Danny Gatton Signature model. Note the double blade Barden pickups and (see below) the angled steel saddles. [photo by Michael Stevens]

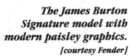

Danny Gatton with his '53 Telecaster...a picture of the past! [photo by John Peden]

The James Burton Signature model with modern paisley graphics. [courtesy Fender]

Michael Stevens (left) and John Page (right) presenting Fender president Bill Schultz with 40th Anniversary model number 001. [courtesy Fender]

Robben Ford on stage in Paris with his Custom Shop Telecaster [photo by Christophe Madronna]

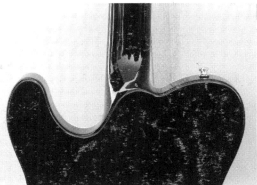

The revolution of the 90s... a Telecaster with a set neck.

The Bajo Sexto,
i.e. a baritone
Telecaster
designed by
Custom Shop
luthier
Fred Stuart.

e Tele Plus with Fender-Lace sensors. [courtesy Fender]

Bob Dylan in 1989 playing a silver Sparkle
Telecaster built by the Custom Shop.
[courtesy Jay Black]

Albert Collins
(a.k.a. Mr. Iceman)
with the 1966
Telecaster Custom
which served as
a basis for his
Signature model.

- the intermediate model is upgraded with an ebony fretboard, a Strat-style tremolo and a Wilkinson Roller Nut;
- the top model has three pickups (two humbuckers and one single coil), an ebony fretboard and a Floyd Rose Pro tremolo.

After many unsuccessful attempts in the past, the Set Neck Telecasters built by the Custom Shop have probably struck the best ever compromise between a Fender and a Gibson.

In less than five years, the new Fender company has completely restored the Telecaster range and opened up a new chapter in the history of America's most enduring solid body. Several variants are currently available to answer the wants and needs of new generations of musicians, playing different styles of music. From the classic 50s reissue to the lavish Set Neck models, there is a Telly for everyone not to mention the superlative guitars built by the Custom Shop (a.k.a.

the dream factory). Only time will tell whether the new Fender company will sustain the momentum it has successfully built since 1985. All those caring for the Fender name and reputation sincerely hope that the company will not be tempted to "sell out" like CBS did a quarter century ago...

Forty years after the Esquire made its official debut at the July 1950 NAMM show, Telecaster guitars are still being made in California. The unprecedented number of variants available today bears testimony that Fender senior solid body is more than ever a major contender in the field of electric guitars. The Telly may not have the flashy appeal of a Stratocaster but it has proved to be the most versatile electric beyond all trends and fashions. Its current popularity on the threshold of the 90s is, among many other lasting achievements, a living tribute to the genius of the late Leo Fender.

United States Patent Office
839,999
Registered Dec. 5, 1967

PRINCIPAL REGISTER
Trademark

Ser. No. 270,196, filed Apr. 28, 1967

Columbia Broadcasting System, Inc. (New York corporation)
51 W. 52nd St.
New York, N.Y.   10019

For: ACOUSTIC AND ELECTRIC GUITARS, in CLASS 36.
First use at least as early as 1961; in commerce at least as early as 1961.

C. A. MARLOW, *Examiner.*

Combined affadavit under Sec. 8 and 15 accepted and filed 11/28/73

NOTES

Excerpts from a conversation between George Fullerton and Dave Crocker (May 1991): 1-2-9-12-13

Quote from a Leo Fender interview in *Rolling Stone* magazine (February 1976): 3

Excerpts from conversations between Freddie Tavares and author (January 1988): 4-10-15-20-22

Quotes from a Leo Fender interview in *Guitar Player* magazine (May 1978): 5-6-7-11

Quote from a Leo Fender interview in *International Musician* magazine (March 1978): 8

Quote from a Leo Fender interview in *Guitar Player* magazine (October 1984): 14

Quote from a Don Randall interview in *Guitar Player* (July 1978): 16

Excerpt from *Musical Merchandise* review (August 1950): 17

Quote from a Don Randall interview in *Music Industry* (June 1955): 18

Excerpts from a conversation between George Fullerton and author (January 1988): 19

Excerpt from a conversation between Bill Carson and author (January 1988): 21

Excerpts from conversations between Dan Smith and author (January 1988 & November 1990): 23-24-25-26-28-29

Quote from a Bill Schultz interview in *Musical Merchandise* review (March 1985): 27

The first prototype built by Leo Fender in late 1949
[courtesy John Hanley/photo by Dave Crocker]

Exceedingly rare two-pickup Esquire from mid-1950 (#0013). Note absence of "skunk stripe" on back of the neck.
[photo by Kerry Wetzel]

Two-pickup Esquire (#0087) custom-built for country artist Hal Hart. The black-lacquered body is made of pinewood.

1950 Broadcaster (#0027) *[photo by John Peden]*

The March 1953 Telecaster (a.k.a. Nancy) of the late Roy Buchan[an]
[courtesy John Sprung & Gil Southworth/ photo by John Spr[ung]]

The specific wiring circuit of the early Tellies. Note brown resistor soldered to the switch and orange sheath. [photo by John Sprung]

The figured ash body of a 1953 Telecaster adequately showcased by the butterscotch blond finish.
[courtesy Jeffrey Gray]

1951 "No-Caster," i.e. trans[ition] model between the Broadcaster [and] the Telecaster. [courtesy Jeffrey]

1952 Esquire with original custom copper finish.
[courtesy Jim Colclasure/photo by Kathy Ketner]

1956 Telecaster (#12049) painted with ultra-rare red custom finish. [courtesy Cliff Williams/photo by Pete Alenov]

This 1957 Telecaster is factory-finished with an original 2-tone sunburst over its ash body. [courtesy Jeffrey Gray]

Mid-56 Esquire in a very unusual pale green finish. Note the absence of a string guide on headstock. [courtesy Cliff Williams/photo by John Peden]

Mid-1955 Telecaster with flat poles on lead pickup. [photo by Patrick Selmer]

1958 Telecaster in typical late 50s blond finish. [courtesy Gil Southworth/photo by Debbie Mazzoleni]

Left-handed 1960 Telecaster in Custom Ducco red finish. [courtesy Don's Musicland/ photo by Sutter's Arts]

1961 Esquire. Note single ply pickguard. [courtesy Jeffrey Gray]

1960 Lake Placid Blue Telecaster. This particular instrument belonged to Alvino Rey, well-known Fender endorser during the 50s and 60s. [courtesy Jeffrey Gray]

1960 Esquire C [courtesy Gil South

One of the very first Telecaster Custom (#38820) with top loading bridge and body marking. Also note distinct 3-tone sunburst and 3-ply pickguard with 5 mounting screws. [courtesy Jeffrey Gray]

'63 mahogany-bodied Telecaster [photo by John Peden]

1966-67 custom colour chart

This August 1964 Telecaster Custom with gold sparkle finish and maple board was custom-built for famous country performer Buck Owens.

1963 Telecaster Custom
[courtesy Gil Southworth/photo by Debbie Mazzoleni]

'63 Telecaster with "unlisted" purple sparkle custom finish.

39

1969 Telecaster
Thinline in natural
mahogany finish.
[courtesy Jim Colclasure/
photo by Kathy Ketner]

Experimental
hollow body
Telecaster from
1967 with bound
spruce top and
rosewood back.
[courtesy Albert Molinaro]

1967 Telecaster Custom [courtesy Didier Colombi]

1969 Telecaster with
(faded) Paisley Red finish
[photo by John Sprung]

Show-stopper in "day-glo" finish specially made for a 1968 trade convention.
Note silver paint underneath see-through pickguard to conceal top routing.
[courtesy Margie Baker & Jim Colclasure]

9 Telecaster Thinline finished in
ery unusual canary yellow colour.
artesy Cliff Williams/photo by Pete Alenov]

A fairly rare 1967
Telecaster Custom with
double black binding.

Gold sparkle 1967 Telecaster.
[courtesy Gil Southworth]

8 Blue Flower Telecaster [courtesy Gil Southworth]

Candy Apple Red 1967 Telecaster
factory-equipped with
Bigsby vibrato tailpiece.
[courtesy Didier Colombi]

1969 Esquire with Maple Neck. [photo by Debbie Mazzoleni]

1971 Rosewood Telecaster with stunning grain pattern [courtesy Gil Southworth/ photo by Debbie Mazzoleni]

More naturals (part 1)... Zebrawood Telecaster prototype [photo by John Sprung]

More naturals (part 2)... one-off all-maple show sample [photo by John Sprung]

Thinline with humbuckers (type II) and factory Bigsby. [courtesy Albert Molinaro]

1972 Telecaster Custom. One of the very last Customs built with a bound body prior to the model's reshuffle. [courtesy Dave Kenney]

Contrary to what this picture might suggest, Antigua Telecasters don't grow in trees! [courtesy Gil Southworth/photo by Debbie Mazzoleni]

1975 regular Telecaster with 3-tone sunburst [courtesy Guitar Express]

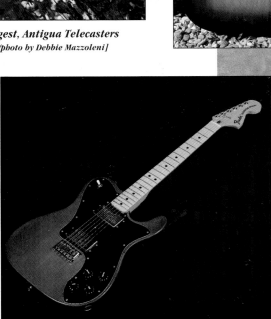

The first Deluxe off the production line. This guitar is stamped with serial number 000001 and a December 1972 marking on the neck. [photo by John Sprung]

The revamped Telecaster Custom introduced in 1972. Note Tilt Neck bullet above the nut, front humbucker and modified pickguard assembly with 4 controls. [courtesy Albert Molinaro]

1974 Telecaster Deluxe with Strat-style tremolo tailpiece.
[courtesy Guitar Express/photo by Debbie Mazzoleni]

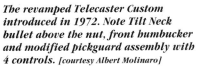

Walnut Elite Telecaster with ebony fretboard [courtesy Fend

1952 reissue model (a.k.a. the Vintage Telecaster)
[courtesy Fender]

*Left-banded 1983
Elite Telecaster*
[courtesy Buck Sulcer/photo
by Debbie Mazzoleni]

*1981 Standard model in
Pewter* [courtesy Albert Molinaro]

*Revamped 1983
Standard model with
Elite bridge saddles.*
[courtesy Albert Molinaro]

*1981 Black & Gold Telecaster. Note the special
design 6-piece bridge assembly in gold-plated
brass.* [courtesy Fender]

1988 American Standard
[courtesy Fender]

40th Anniversary
Telecaster in
Antique Sunburst.
This particular
instrument is the
first one built by the
Custom Shop in 1988.
[courtesy Fender]

*...: James Burton signature model in black with
...d Paisley graphics. Bottom: early pre-series
...rton in Frost Red with black chrome parts.*

**Limited series Shoreline Gold
Thinline from the Custom Shop. Note
abalone dot markers inlaid into the
fretboard.** [courtesy Fender]

45

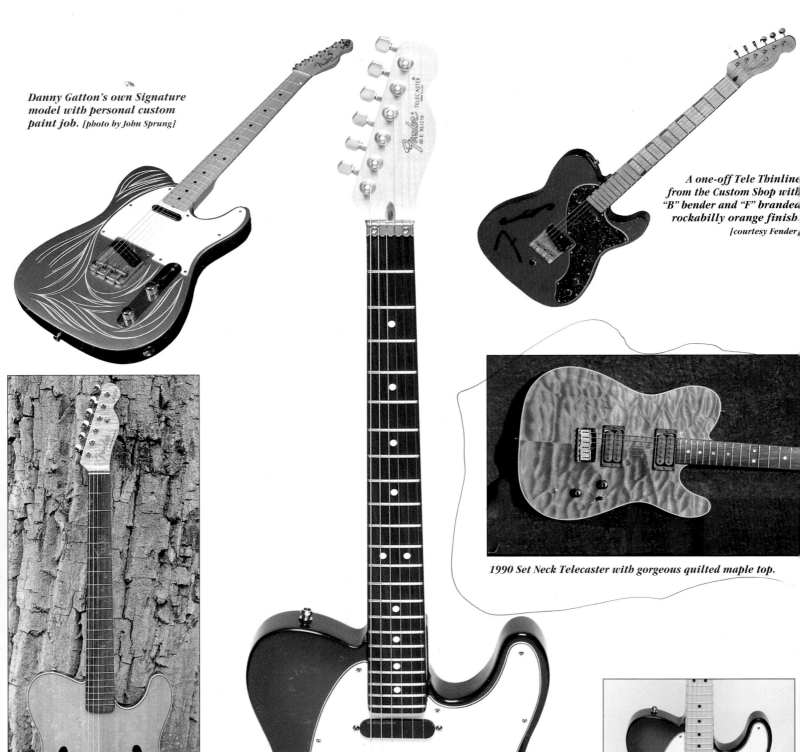

Danny Gatton's own Signature model with personal custom paint job. [photo by John Sprung]

A one-off Tele Thinline from the Custom Shop with "B" bender and "F" branded rockabilly orange finish. [courtesy Fender]

1990 Set Neck Telecaster with gorgeous quilted maple top.

Double f-hole custom Esquire (a.k.a. Page-O-Caster) custom built in 1990 as 40th anniversary Esquire for the author. [photo by Patrick Selmer]

1990 Deluxe Tele Plus with tremolo system and roller nut [courtesy Fender]

Tele Plus in Blue Frost [courtesy Fender]

LIST PRICE 1951-1991

DATE	MODEL	PRICE	DATE	MODEL	PRICE	DATE	MODEL	PRICE
July 1951	Telecaster	$189.50	February 1972	Rosewood	$399.50	January 1984	Walnut Elite	$1199.00
	Esquire	$149.50		Thinline (II)	$375.00		Gold Elite	$1059.00
	+case $39.95			Telecaster Custom	$315.00		Elite	$899.00
				Telecaster (R/W)	$283.00		Vintage Telecaster	$899.00
February 1957	Telecaster	$199.50		+case $65.00			Standard (M/N)	$589.00
	Esquire	$164.50		(5)			(7)(8)	
	+case $49.50		January 1973	Deluxe (non trem.)	$399.50	January 1985	Walnut Elite	$799.00
	(1)			Thinline (II)	$375.00		Gold Elite	$699.00
January 1960	Telecaster Custom	$239.50		Custom (II)	$315.00		Elite	$599.00
	Telecaster	$209.50		Telecaster (R/W)	$283.00		Vintage Reissue	$749.00
	Esquire Custom	$199.50		+case $65.00			Standard (M/N)	$469.00
	Esquire	$169.50		(5)			(6)(7)	
	+case $52.50		March 1974	Deluxe	$410.00	January 1986	Vintage Telecaster	$799.00
	(1)(2)			Thinline (II)	$385.00		(7)	
July 1966	Telecaster Custom	$232.00		Custom (II)	$325.00	March 1987	Vintage Telecaster	$849.99
	Telecaster	$203.00		Telecaster (R/W)	$295.00		(7)	
	Esquire Custom	$194.00		+case $67.00		October 1987	Vintage Telecaster	$899.99
	Esquire	$164.00		(5)			(7)	
	+case $52.50		November 1976	Deluxe	$490.00	January 1988	Vintage Reissue	$899.99
	(1)(2)			Thinline (II)	$475.00		American Std	$599.99
October 1966	Telecaster Custom	$244.50		Custom (II)	$405.00		(6)(7)	
	Telecaster	$214.50		Telecaster (R/W)	$370.00	October 1988	Vintage Reissue	$999.99
	Esquire Custom	$209.50		+case $70.00			American Std	$649.99
	Esquire	$179.50		(5)(6)			(6)(7)	
	+case $57.50		December 1977	Deluxe	$565.00	January 1989	Vintage Reissue	$999.99
	(1)(2))			Thinline (II)	$555.00		American Std	$689.99
July 1968	Thinline	$319.50		Custom (II)	$475.00		(6)(7)	
	Paisley/Flower	$279.50		Telecaster (R/W)	$440.00	November 1989	Vintage Reissue	$1099.99
	Telecaster Custom	$259.50		+case $65.00			American Std	$699.99
	Telecaster	$229.50		(5)(6)			(6)(7)	
	Esquire Custom	$224.50	September 1979	Deluxe	$685.00	January 1990	James Burton	TBA
	Esquire	$194.50		Custom (II)	$580.00		Vintage Reissue	$1099.99
	+case $57.50			Telecaster (R/W)	$535.00		American Std	$739.99
	(1)(2)(3)(4)			+case $110.00			(6)(7)	
May 1969	Rosewood	$375.50		(5)(6)		June 1990	James Burton	$1299.99
	Thinline	$356.50	September 1980	Deluxe	$750.00		Vintage Reissue	$1099.99
	Paisley/Flower	$299.50		Custom (II)	$675.00		Deluxe Tele Plus	$999.99
	Telecaster Custom	$299.50		Telecaster (R/W)	$635.00		Tele Plus	$899.99
	Telecaster	$269.50		+case $125.00			American Std	$739.99
	Esquire Custom	$259.50		(6)			Danny Gatton	$2400.00
	Esquire	$224.50	December 1981	Black & Gold	$880.00		Albert Collins	$2400.00
	+case $62.50			Vintage Reissue	$875.00		(6)(7)	
	(1)(2)(3)(4)			Telecaster	$780.00			
March 1970	Rosewood	$395.00		(7)(8)		January 1991	Set-Neck (3pu's)	$1949.99
	Thinline	$375.00	June 1982	Black & Gold	$925.00		Set-Neck (trem.)	$1749.99
	Telecaster Custom	$315.00		Vintage Reissue	$875.00		Set-Neck	$1649.99
	Telecaster (R/W)	$283.00		Telecaster	$820.00		James Burton	$1299.99
	+case $65.00			(7)(8)			Vintage Reissue	$1099.99
	(6)		July 1983	Walnut Elite	$1195.00		Deluxe Tele Plus	$1069.99
January 1971	Thinline	$375.00		Gold Elite	$1055.00		Tele Plus	$969.99
	Telecaster Custom	$315.00		Elite	$895.00		American Std	$779.99
	Telecaster (R/W)	$283.00		Vintage Reissue	$895.00		Danny Gatton	$2400.00
	+case $65.00			Standard (M/N)	$550.00		Albert Collins	$2400.00
	(5)			(7)(8)			(6)(7)	

NOTES: (1) custom finish: +5% (2) left-handed: +10% (3) maple fretboard: +5% (4) Bigsby tremolo: $55.00 (5) specific price according to appointments (6) choice of standard finishes (7) case included (8) custom finish: $75/$100

THE TELECASTER IN DETAIL

Players and collectors are aware that a number of features may actually differentiate the same Telecaster variant over the years. Therefore, the purpose of this chapter is to examine in greater detail the guitar's major components and to describe how they have evolved since the 1950s. This information will contribute to selecting useful criteria for both dating and authenticating Telecasters and Esquires.

THE NECK

HEADSTOCK DECAL

As is typical of Fender electrics, Telecasters and Esquires are branded with a decal applied on the headstock. Provided this decal is original, the Fender logo and its assorted markings may help narrow down the period of issue of a guitar. Having said that, it should be borne in mind that changes usually occurred over a period of time, during which two types of decals overlapped.

- **THE BROADCASTER**

The decal features the original Fender logo (a.k.a. "spaghetti" logo) in silver with a black trim and the model's name in thin black script between inverted commas. When FENDER had to surrender the designation in February 1951, the "Broadcaster" name was simply clipped off of the decal, then applied with only the Fender spaghetti logo. These "NO-CASTER" decals may be found on dual pickup guitars made until Summer 1951.

- **THE TELECASTER**

From Summer 1951 right up to the end of 1965, the decal featured the silver spaghetti logo and the model's name in thin black script between inverted commas. After late 1961, it was completed with 3 patent numbers below the word Telecaster, i.e.
DES 164,227 PAT. 2,573,254 2,784,631

In early 1966, the decal first incorporated the modern Fender logo in gold with a black trim (a.k.a. "transition" logo) and only two patent numbers, i.e.
PAT. 2,573,254 3,143,028

By Fall 1967, new markings appeared with a black Fender logo with a gold trim (a.k.a. CBS logo) and a significantly enlarged model's name in bolder lettering. The two patent numbers previously mentioned were retained, but shifted below the Fender logo. In late 1976, the patent numbers were deleted when FENDER first displayed the serial number on the headstock's decal.

In mid-1983, a slightly downsized silver logo with a black trim was introduced on the Elite and Standard Telecasters. At the same time FENDER reverted to a smaller black lettering for the model's designation. This logo is still a current feature of early 90s production models such as the American Standard, the Tele Plus or the James Burton.

- **THE TELECASTER CUSTOM**

The very first Custom models made in mid-1959 may be found with a regular Telecaster decal without any "Custom" mention. Most 1959 guitars, though, display a decal with a gold spaghetti logo whilst the model's designation actually reads "Custom Telecaster" (and NOT Telecaster Custom!) with a slightly bolder script – albeit not as tall – than the lettering on the regular Telecaster. Besides, it is not set between inverted commas.

In mid-1964, a new decal appeared with a gold "transition" logo and 3 patent numbers, identical to those displayed at the same period on the regular Telecaster, i.e.
DES 164,227 PAT. 2,573,254 2,784,631

but it kept the previous "Custom Telecaster" mention and script style. In the course of 1968, probably on standardisation grounds, the regular Telecaster's decal with the CBS black logo and 2 patent numbers, but without any "Custom" mention, was gradually applied.

After mid-1972, the Custom designation referred to a totally different guitar with a humbucker in the neck position. FENDER kept the same basic decal, i.e. black logo, enlarged Telecaster name and 2 patent numbers, but a "Custom" label in black fancy lettering was added below Telecaster. In late 1976, the patent numbers were deleted and replaced by the serial number, whilst the Custom label was redesigned to feature a straighter script. The model was discontinued in 1981 with this decal.

- **THE TELECASTER THINLINE**

The original 1968 issue is fitted with the same decal as the regular model of the same period, i.e. CBS black logo, enlarged Telecaster script and 2 patent numbers, but no specific "Thinline" marking on the headstock. When the model was revamped with humbuckers in late 1971, a "Thinline" mention in black lettering was added on the upper bout of the headstock. In late 1976, the patent numbers were deleted and replaced by the serial number. No other changes took place until the Thinline was discontinued in 1979.

- **THE TELECASTER DELUXE**

While catalogued, the model was always fitted with the same decal featuring a CBS black logo with the name in bold black letters as per a curved line. No patent numbers were ever mentioned on its headstock, but in late 1976 the serial number was added to the decal.

- **THE VINTAGE TELECASTER**

The '52 reissue is naturally fitted with a 50s style decal, but the spaghetti logo has a fractionnally bigger lettering with a thicker black trim than a real 1952 issue.

- **THE ESQUIRE**

The decal of the senior member of the family initially featured a silver spaghetti logo with the model's name in thin black lettering between inverted commas. By 1952, the single pickup version came out with a gold spaghetti logo, but silver was reinstated in mid-55. In 1963 the decal was completed with the 3 patent numbers found since late 1961 on the regular Telecaster headstock, i.e.
DES 164,227 PAT. 2,573,254 2,784,631

After mid-1967, a decal incorporating a gold transition logo appeared whilst the number of patents displayed was simultaneously reduced from 3 to 2, i.e.
PAT. 2,573,254 3,143,028

In the latter part of 1968, the decal was again modified to feature the CBS black logo and a significantly enlarged model name whilst the 2 patent numbers were relocated below the Fender logo. The Esquire was discontinued with these headstock markings on the threshold of the 1970s.

- **THE ESQUIRE CUSTOM**

Like its Telecaster counterpart, the very first Esquire Customs from mid-1959 may be found with a regular Esquire decal featuring a silver spaghetti logo but no "Custom" marking. Very soon, though, a specific decal was introduced with a gold spaghetti logo and "Custom Esquire" (NOT Esquire Custom) in slightly bolder black lettering without inverted commas.

Owing to a fairly limited production, the model kept its original headstock markings (without patent numbers) until the late 60s, before FENDER

THE *Fender* TELECASTER

'52 Telecaster

'58 Telecaster

'63 Custom

'65 Telecaster

'66 Custom

'69 Telecaster

'70 Rosewood

'73 Telecaster

'74 Deluxe

'75 Thinline

'78 Custom

'83 Vintage

'83 Elite

'88 American Std

'90 Set-Neck

'50 Esquire

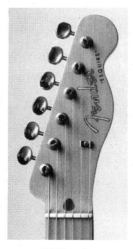

'58 Esquire

'60 Esquire Custom

'66 Esquire

'69 Esquire

49

switched over to a black logo with a much bigger Esquire script and 2 patent numbers, i.e.
PAT. 2,573,254 3,143,028

The Esquire Custom was discontinued in late 1969 with these headstock markings.

Also worth mentioning:

- Up to 1956 the headstock decal is positioned between the nut and the string retainer next to the G-string tuning post.

- Beginning in 1956, the string retainer is placed closer to the nut, roughly in the alignment of the A-string tuning post, and the decal thus relocated on the upper bout of the headstock.

- The black logo with enlarged markings was apparently introduced by CBS to make the Fender brand more conspicuous on television at a time when rock music was getting heavier exposure on the screen.

- Since the advent of the black logo in the late 60s, a small circled "R" (for registered) has always been featured right behind Fender on the headstock decal. More recently, the same registered marking has been added behind the Telecaster name on full production models.

- The Rosewood Telecaster simply featured a modern silver logo with a black trim and no model designation or patent numbers.

- From 1950 up to 1968 the headstock decal was always featured over the finishing lacquer. With the introduction of polyester finishes in the late 60s, the decal was affixed before the finishing coat and thus sealed under it, to provide a more durable branding. Accordingly, FENDER then used a new type of reverse decal known as "C transfer" and requiring a special solvent for its application. Today, only the Vintage models have a headstock decal applied over the finishing lacquer.

- With the relocation of serial numbers on the headstock in late 1976, patent numbers were deleted from the decal and the words "MADE IN U.S.A." added below the model's designation.

FRETBOARD MATERIAL

A distinctive feature in terms of sound, feel and looks. As a quick rule of thumb, a maple fretboard contributes to a brighter sound than rosewood, all else being equal.

- From 1950 up to mid-1959, Telecaster guitars were exclusively fitted with a fretted one-piece maple neck (Maple Neck hereafter) without a separate fingerboard.

- By mid-1959, the original Maple Neck was replaced by a rosewood-capped neck. The first variant made between mid-59 and mid-62 is characterized by a fretboard milled flat on the neck base and thus quite thick, hence its "slab board" nickname among collectors. After July 1962, a curved rosewood fretboard (i.e.with a convex base) superseded the slab board. At first, the rosewood cap was kept fairly thick, but in 1963 it was gradually engineered into a thinner veneer which would remain as the standard feature for the next 20 years.

- In January 1967 a maple fingerboard officially became optional on most Fender electrics, but Telecaster guitars with a maple-capped neck were actually available well before 1967, either on a replacement or a custom order basis. The 2-piece maple neck from the 60s is easily distinguished from the original one-piece neck by both the lack of walnut plug above the nut and contrasting stripe (a.k.a. "skunk stripe") on the back.

- In early 1969 the original style one-piece Maple Neck was reissued as an option on Telecasters and Esquires in lieu of the 2-piece neck with a separate maple cap. By 1970, both rosewood board neck and Maple Neck became a standard appointment on Telecaster guitars, but not at the same price!

- In mid-1983, the curved rosewood board in use since 1963 was discontinued and replaced by a new cap milled flat on the neck base. This new type of slab board, then designed to match the novel Biflex truss-rod then introduced on the Elite and Standard Telecasters, is still the regular mount on early 90s production models.

Also worth mentioning:

- The original Maple Neck from the 50s is sealed with clear cellulose lacquer (often yellowed with age) whilst the post-69 version is finished with polyester and more recently polyurethane, except on the '52 Vintage reissue. Since late 1987, FENDER has introduced a clear satin finish on Maple Necks sealed with polyurethane.

- In the early 60s a few instruments were produced with a cocoa bolo fretboard in lieu of rosewood. Likewise, hickory was also occasionally used for necks instead of maple.

- Production Rosewood Telecasters were made with a one-piece rosewood neck, but George Harrison's guitar came with a 2-piece rosewood neck.

- During the 70s, the regular and the Custom Telecasters could be ordered with either a rosewood board or a Maple Neck, but the Deluxe and the Thinline type II were exclusively fitted with a Maple Neck.

- The 1983 Walnut Elite Telecaster was fitted with an ebony fretboard, then considered by FENDER to be more appropriate for fingering than walnut.

- The 40th Anniversary Telecaster was exclusively offered with a one-piece Maple Neck

- The recent Set Neck Telecaster has a mahogany neck reinforced with an inner maple core strip and is fitted with either a rosewood or an ebony board.

- Until the early 80s, Fender necks were cut on a pin-router and therefore they display two characteristic small holes at both ends, one on the underface of the heel and one on the back of the peghead between the holes drilled for the D and G tuners.

POSITION MARKERS

On Telecaster guitars, whether with a 21 or a 22-fret neck, position markers are materialized by dots whose material and spacing at the 12th fret changed over the years.

- 50s Maple Necks are inlaid with black dots (diameter=1/4") which in 1950 originally showed a 5/8" spacing at the 12th fret. By the end of 1952, though, the 12th fret spacing was widened by 3/16" and the double dots became neatly crossed by the A and B strings.

- 1959 rosewood-capped necks were initially inlaid with matt whitish dots, known as "clay dots," which kept the same 12th fret spacing as the post-52 Maple Necks. But, in mid-1963, FENDER reverted to the original 5/8" narrower spacing for the 12th fret dots, whether on rosewood or maple-capped necks.

- In early 1965, clay dots were superseded by slightly bigger pearloid dots, which subsequently remained the standard trim on rosewood-capped necks until mid-1983.

- By mid-1983, pearloid dots were dropped and replaced by matt white dots on the newer style rosewood slab board. This combination is still the current trim on early 90s production models.

Also worth mentioning:

- Matt white dots were first used on the '62-style Vintage reissue models (Stratocaster, P.Bass and J.Bass) as a modern counterpart of the original clay dots.

- The 40th Anniversary Telecaster is fitted with dots made of abalone, also currently found on some Custom Shop models.

- Despite their 22-fret neck, the American Standard and Tele Plus feature the same basic dot marker configuration.

- The fretboard markers are matched by side dots, which are black on Maple Necks and whitish (also black in the 70s) on rosewood-capped necks. On the latter, the side dots generally sit astride board and neck, except on 70s models where they are inserted beside the fretboard.

NUT	**12TH FRET DOTS**

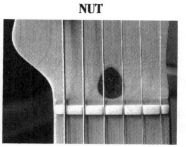

50s Maple Neck

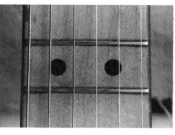

50-52 black dots

original "spaghetti" logo

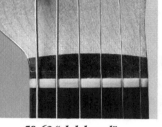

59-62 "slab board"

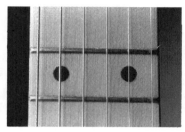

53-59 black dots

mid-60s transition logo

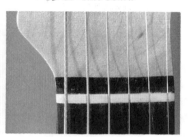

63-83 curved board

59-63 clay dots

CBS black Logo

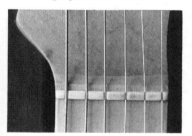

63-69 maple board

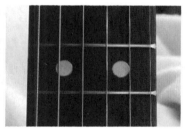

63-65 clay dots

modern silver logo

71-81 Tilt Neck

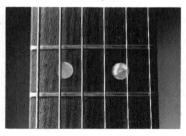

65-83 pearl dots

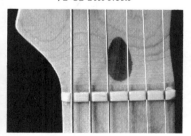

modern Maple Neck

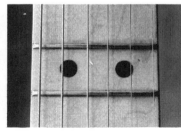

modern black dots

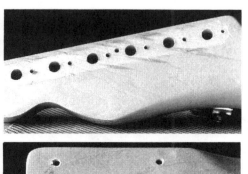

Pin router's holes are located on the back of the headstock and underneath the neck's heel.

80s Biflex neck

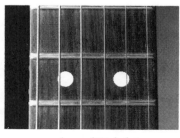

modern whitish dots

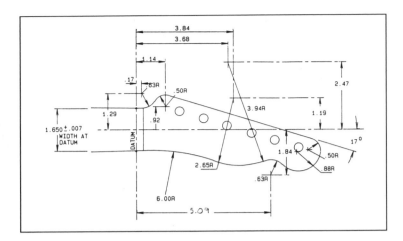

TRUSS ROD

With the notable exception of the recent Set Neck model, all Telecasters and Esquires are equipped with a detachable bolt-on neck, but they do not share the same truss-rod installation and adjustment system.

- The neck of the earliest 1950 models is deprived of any reinforcing truss-rod. Only a handful were made and they can primarily be identified by the lack of truss-rod bolt at the heel, as well as the absence of contrasting stripe on the back.

- By Fall 1950, the Broadcaster's neck was fitted with a metal rod inserted from the rear via a channel routed in the back spine. This explains why one-piece Maple Necks have a "skunk" stripe on the back (to fill the channel) and a plug above the nut (to fill the anchoring point of the rod). Adjustment of the rod is achieved by a bolt (slothead until early '51, Phillips head thereafter) located in the neck heel, whilst pitch can only be modified by inserting little shims in the neck pocket.

- The advent of a separate rosewood fretboard brought about a change in the truss-rod installation. With a 2-piece neck, it is easier to drill the rod channel in the neck prior to glueing the fretboard and thus rosewood-capped necks do not have a back stripe or a plug above the nut. The installation from the front did not warrant any modification in the neck adjustment.

- 60s maple-capped necks also have the truss rod inserted from the front and, like rosewood-capped necks, they do not have a contrasting back stripe or a plug above the nut. From a purist's point of view, they should not be referred to as "Maple Necks" (which somehow implies the notion of a one-piece neck), but as "maple board" necks.

- The original style one-piece Maple Neck with a rear installation was reissued in early 1969 on Telecaster guitars. By then, FENDER would have had to deal with 2 methods of installation of the truss rod, i.e. from the front and from the rear. On standardisation grounds, it was decided to retain only the installation from the rear, and this is why rosewood-capped necks made after Spring 1969 usually feature a contrasting back stripe and a plug above the nut.

- The Tilt Neck was never fitted to regular Telecasters, but it became a standard appointment on the other variants from the 70s, i.e. the Custom, the Thinline type II and the Deluxe. The Tilt Neck incorporates two functions:

  - truss-rod adjustment via a wrench inserted into a metal bullet located above the nut

  - neck angle adjustment via a smaller wrench inserted into the hole below the lower screw of the neck plate

Otherwise its most (in)famous characteristic is a 3-bolt fastening system, as opposed to the traditional Fender 4-bolt mounting. Instruments equipped with a Tilt Neck do not have a bolt on the front heel of the neck (like other Fender guitars) but they display a circular metal plate underneath the heel base and in the neck pocket. Despite theses changes, the truss-rod was still inserted from the rear, hence a back stripe. By 1981, Telecaster variants equipped with a Tilt Neck were all discontinued and Leo Fender's device was abandoned.

- In early 1983, FENDER introduced its Biflex truss rod, which is basically an improved Tilt Neck, albeit with a classic 4-bolt neck mounting. The Biflex rod can be adjusted in two directions (for concave and convex bows) via a bolt buried in a small well above the nut, whilst the neck pitch is set up with a wrench inserted into the neck plate. It was first fitted to the 1983 Elite and Standard models, but since then it has been also built into all the production Telecasters (bar the Vintage reissue) made in Corona since 1986.

Also worth mentioning:

- On the rosewood-capped prototypes from 1959, the truss-rod was still inserted from the rear and not from the front. This explains why 1959-60 catalogues show pictures of Telecaster guitars with a plug above the nut.

- the Tilt Neck was primarily aimed at upper range models and this may explain why it was never fitted to the regular Telecaster, which FENDER wanted to keep "as is."

FRETBOARD RADIUS

- Older Fender guitars are known to have a slightly convex fretboard compared to the much flatter board of, say, a Gibson guitar, and until the early 70s all Telecaster necks were designed with a basic 7.25" fretboard radius.

The 1973 Deluxe was the first model to offer a slightly flatter 9.5" radius, whilst other Telecaster variants kept a standard fingerboard. In 1983, the newer Elite and Standard Telecasters came out with an even flatter 12" radius, meant to facilitate string bending. Current production models have come back to an intermediate 9.5" radius, except the Vintage Telecaster (7.25") and the Set Neck Telecaster (12").

- Thin fretwire remained a standard feature on Fender guitars for almost 3 decades, although some instruments were first produced with jumbo fretwire in the mid-60s right after the CBS take-over. In 1973, the Telecaster Deluxe was equipped with wider frets to match its flatter fingerboard. By the early 80s, jumbo fretwire became the standard trim, except on the '52 Vintage Reissue which has obviously retained a more traditional thinner fretwire.

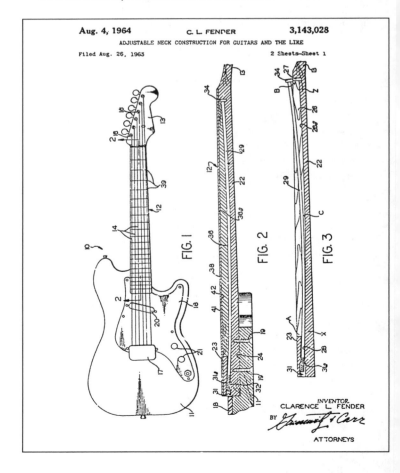

NECK PROFILE

Owing to the amount of manual handwork which took place in the final shaping of necks over the past decades, it is difficult to make sweeping statements about neck profiles. Besides, the way a neck actually feels may be a matter of a few fractions of an inch in the cross section or in the shoulders. More consistent profiles definitely appeared with the introduction in 1981 of sophisticated machinery such as the Austrian-made Zuckerman carving machine, which shapes eight identical necks at a time as per a master template. Therefore, the following indications should serve only as broad guidelines to appreciate the various patterns of Telecaster necks.

- The earliest necks made in 1950 (e.g. Broadcaster) have a pronounced V-shape and their thickness is usually close to one inch. If one takes the 1st and 12th fret as a reference for the cross-section, .95" and 1.00" would be a good average indication for the period. By early 1951, necks became more rounded and less "Veed" with slight variations in thickness, e.g. .90" and 1.00" on a '52 Telly, but overall kept a similar cross-section until the mid-50s.

- V necks (a.k.a. "boat necks") reappeared in the course of 1955 and became a standard pattern over 1956 and 1957, with a variable cross-section ranging between, say, anything like .86"/.94" at the 1st fret and .97"/1.02" at the 12th fret. Early 1958 necks usually still have a slight V feel, but a much flatter profile was quickly adopted with measurements steadily below .90" at the 1st fret and 1.00" at the 12th fret. Rosewood necks made after mid-59 show a really flat pattern with measurements often below .80" and .92".

- Early to mid-60s necks retained similar dimensions, but after 1963 they often feature more shoulders, hence a different feel from a typical 1959-61 neck. By the late 60s, an increased production brought about a tremendous variance in neck profiles and both flat and more chunky configurations may be found. As a rule, however, round clubby necks with a lot of shoulders are the norm on most 70s Telecaster guitars with measurements like .85" at the 1st fret and .95" at the 12th fret.

- As previously indicated, the acquisition of duplicating machines helped FENDER to standardize neck profiles. In line with contemporary players' requirements, a rather flat profile has been selected as the norm on modern Fender guitars. The Vintage reissue has purposely kept a slightly thicker cross-section (.82"/.87") than other production guitars which feature a gentle "C" profile (.80"/.87").

THE BODY

WOOD MATERIAL

Although other timbers have been used at times, ash is the wood most commonly found on bodies. Because of its heavy grain, it was ideally suited to the semi-transparent blond finish which was the standard finish on Telecaster guitars between 1950 and 1981. Oddly enough, when describing Telecasters and Esquires, Fender commercial brochures scarcely made a clear reference to the type of body wood. During the 50s, catalogues simply mentioned that "the body is made of fine clear hardwood" and subsequent brochures pretty much followed suit.

Ash is a fairly inconsistent timber and its weight can vary in substantial proportions, which explain why some ash-bodied guitars seem to weigh a ton when others may appear as light as a feather. Its final density depends both on where the tree grows and which portion of the tree is used to cut the body.

As a quick rule of thumb, suffice it to say that the more water (rain) is absorbed by the tree, the lighter the eventual wood spread. Conversely, the bottom portion of the tree usually absorbs more water, particularly during winter, than the top portion. When saturated with water the grain gets wider but, as the water recedes under warmer weather, the wood dries out and becomes much lighter. All in all, obtaining light and figured ash (called "swamp ash" or "punk ash") is not a question of luck, but simply a matter of specifications (and price) when ordering wood from a timber merchant. Over the years, weight was not necessarily a prime consideration when procuring ash and this certainly explains why FENDER received wood spreads of variable density.

By and large, 50s ash bodies are lighter on the average than their 60s and 70s counterparts, even though some Broadcasters and black guard Tellies are indeed quite heavy. The density of ash purchased in the mid-60s is probably one of the major reasons behind the scooped-out Thinline model, at a time when FENDER was commercially keen to produce lighter guitars. Light-weight bodies are fairly hard to come by in the 70s and early 80s, but recently FENDER has paid more attention to this important characteristic.

Otherwise, contrary to popular belief, ash bodies (even the old ones from the 50s) are usually made of two or even three pieces of wood and one-piece bodies are exceptional. This feature may be revealed by carefully checking the body cross-section, but employees in the spray booth generally took trouble to add extra coats of paint on the body sides to camouflage visible "seams" between planks. Besides, older bodies sanded off show that the pieces are often painstakingly bookmatched to harmonize the grain pattern. As a matter of fact, diagonal seams across the entire body are not unusal on 50s guitars.

Although prominently used over four decades, ash is not the only timber found on production guitars.

- The single pickup black Esquire tentatively introduced in 1950 was most probably built with a pinewood body, like some of the early prototypes crafted by Leo Fender in late 1949.

- In 1956, FENDER switched over to alder for the sunburst Stratocaster and therefore it was quite logical to use this timber on the Custom variant introduced in 1959. Some "custom coloured" instruments were produced with a bound ash body during the 60s, but until 1972 most Customs were fitted with an alder body.

- Likewise, alder was also used during the 60s on regular Telecasters and Esquires finished in sunburst, whilst the (rare) late 50s sunburst models were made with an ash body.

- Up to the early 70s, alder is primarily found on "custom-coloured" guitars where a heavy grain pattern is of no benefit under an opaque finish.

- In the early 60s, Telecaster guitars were momentarily offered with an optional mahogany body and a reddish finish. This variant, available on special order, was prominently displayed in the 1963-64-65 catalogues but it was not produced in large quantitites.

- In 1968 mahogany made a return on the Thinline model, also offered with a natural ash finish, but it was phased out in the early 70s. A few Thinlines type II (with humbuckers) were nevertheless produced with a mahogany body.

- On the more exotic note, rosewood was (obviously) used on the Rosewood Telecaster produced over 1969-72, but a few prototypes were also made in Zebrawood as well as with an all-maple body construction.

- In the 70s, FENDER occasionally resorted to other timbers, such as hackberry wood, in lieu of ash on Telecasters

- The upper grade Elite version was built with an American black walnut body.

- After 1985, ash was naturally retained as the staple wood for the Vintage Reissue but FENDER switched over to alder for the American Standard body.

- The limited edition 40th Anniversary was specially built with a light-weight ash body and a bookmatched curly maple top.

OVERALL SHAPE

The advent of new manufacturing techniques played havoc for nearly a decade with the graceful shape of the body upper shoulder. In the early 70s FENDER first acquired numerically controlled routers (NC routers for short) to cut the bodies instead of the traditional pin routers. Both types of equipment were used simultaneously for a couple of years, since FENDER (under CBS's thumb) could not afford then to invest at once in several NC routers. Anyway, as far as 70s Telecaster bodies are concerned, the problem was that the early NC routers were equipped with a cutter whose diameter prevented the forming of the original curve of the upper shoulder, hence a slightly wrong body shape.

The body of the American Standard.

Bodies made between Spring '51 and Summer '69 (left) feature an open channel between the two pickups. This extra routing no longer exists on 70s and early 80s bodies (right). The above examples both belong to Esquires which shared the same body as Telecasters.

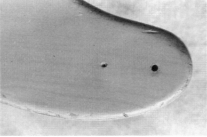

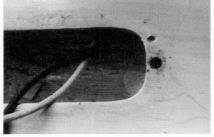

Small clamping boles are typical on most 50s bodies. Top: in the lower born. Bottom: near the control cavity.

The Thinline body is scooped out from the rear and originally featured three pockets as shown in this picture.

Note the difference in the neck pocket between a 50s-60s body (top) and a 70s one (middle). The flatter (and uglier) curve of the upper shoulder on 70s guitars is quite conspicuous in the bottom picture.

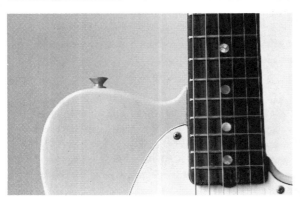

Early 50s bodies feature a prominent lip under the neck beel.

Back contour of a Deluxe body.

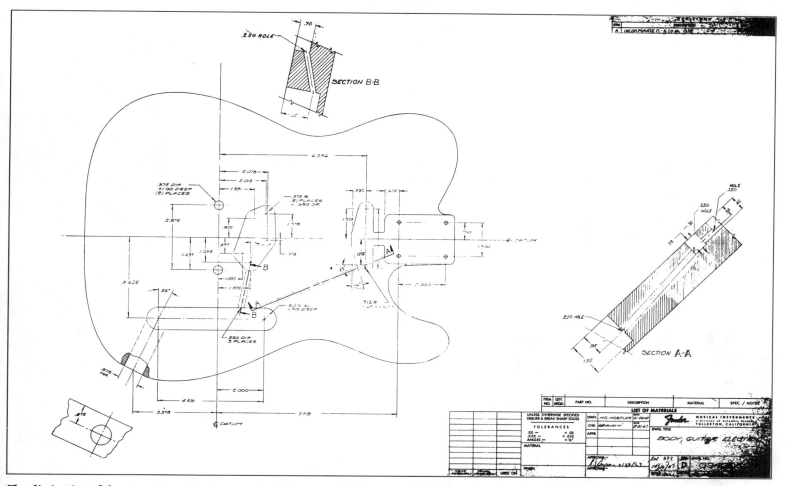

The elimination of the extra top routing between the pickups was first drawn in 1967 as evidenced by this blueprint. [courtesy Fender]

Pictures are better than words to describe what happened and it is best to refer to the photos shown in this book. Suffice it to say that in the 50s and 60s the upper edge of the body blends into the neck at the 17th fret after a fairly steep curve, whilst it joins the neck at the 16th fret after a much flatter curve on most 70s and early 80s models. Besides, on the latter, the neck pocket no longer has the typical "notch" found on the 50s and 60s bodies.

This alteration was not deemed important at the time and for some 9 years Telecaster bodies were produced with a flatter upper shoulder. Simultaneously, the neck pockets also featured two semi-circular notches, reflecting a routing job with a fairly large cutting head. Fortunately, the new senior management brought in by CBS in mid-81 saw the mistake and had the NC router's program and cutter modified!

ROUTINGS & TOOLING MARKS

Routings and tooling marks provide interesting criteria to distinguish the various generations of bodies used on the regular Telecaster and Esquire.

TOP ROUTINGS

• In addition to the neck pocket, the body of the earliest models (Esquire, Broadcaster and "No"Caster) had only three top routings, respectively for the neck pickup, the bridge pickup and the controls.

• Beginning in mid-51 a fourth routing appeared between the neck pickup and the controls cavity. Back in the early 50s, FENDER probably experienced problems in drilling one long channel directly across the hardwood body to house the neck pickup leads into the controls cavity. The intermediate routing was most likely created to allow for the drilling of two shorter channels instead.

• In the late 60s, the availability of sophisticated drilling equipment put an end to the need for an open channel between the neck pickup and the controls

cavity. The modification was first drafted in mid-1967, but the fourth routing was suppressed only in 1969. It was later reintroduced on the Vintage Reissue model and also on the first American Standard guitars. By 1988, though, the routings of the latter were modified to incorporate a single open channel between the neck pickup and the controls cavity.

PIN ROUTER'S HOLES

Although they are usually well patched up and camouflaged, the back of the standard Telecaster bodies feature two small 1/8" holes located:

• between the neck plate and the string ferrules, at a distance of about 3 3/16" from the lower edge of the neck plate

• between the string ferrules and the bottom end of the body, at a distance of about 1" from the bottom end of the body.

These holes ceased to appear after the late 70s when NC routers definitively took over from the old-style pin routers. This being said, they have been maintained on the Vintage Reissue.

CLAMPING HOLES

Older bodies usually feature small clamping holes on the front face, respectively located:

• under the pickguard, between the front pickup and the neck pocket (until the early 60s)

• under the control plate, next to the bottom screw hole of the plate (until the early 60s)

• under the bridge plate, near the upper holes drilled for the strings and the plate screws (until the early 60s)

• under the pickguard, near the extreme pickguard screw hole in the cutaway horn (until the late 50s)

It should be noted that these small holes usually do not show on the late 50s "top loading" models, which have no string holes through the body.

ROUTER'S HUMP

Until about 1964, standard (unbound) bodies show a characteristic side hump next to the neck pocket right at the beginning of the cutaway. This hump, which is perpendicular to the 21st fret, can be clearly felt by moving the finger inside the cutaway. Additionally, it should be mentioned that, on the early 50s guitars, the neck pocket does not perfectly match the shape of the neck heel. In other words, the body forms a protruding "lip" below the neck heel simply because the neck pocket was initially routed with perpendicular sides, without taking into account the fact that the neck heel does not form a right angle. By the mid-50s, the neck pocket was drilled with a slightly smaller angle (90° minus 0.87°) to accomodate the shape of the neck heel.

Also worth mentioning:

• Owing to its peculiar construction, the body of the original Rosewood Telecasters features two maple dowels in the neck pocket (sometimes one) and in the bridge pickup cavity. These dowels were meant to ensure a correct alignment of the hollowed-out body halves sandwiching the thin maple core strip.

• The body of the modern replicas recently built by the Custom Shop do not incorporate such dowels, as Fender luthiers have perfected a new construction method for the Rosewood Telecaster.

PAINTS & FINISHES

Fender finishes can be basically divided in two categories: *"standard"* and *"custom."* Each model has always been offered in one or several characteristic standard finishes available at no extra cost, and anything else, whether listed or not, should be considered as a custom finish.

STANDARD FINISHES

REGULAR TELECASTER & ESQUIRE

• Aside from the black paint tentatively offered on the Esquire in the early 1950 catalogue, Blond(e) remained the sole standard finish between 1950 and 1974.

• By 1975 the distinction between standard and custom finishes was temporarily suspended and the Telecaster became available in 6 stock finishes: Blond, Sunburst, White, Black, Natural and Walnut.

• In 1977 Antigua and Wine (red) were added to the standard finishes but after 1978 the stock palette was gradually narrowed down to 5 finishes as Walnut (in 1978), White (in 1980) and Antigua (in 1980) were phased out.

• In 1981 the notion of "custom finish" was briefly reinstated, but the Telecaster remained available in 6 standard finishes, some old and some new, i.e. Black, Natural, Artic White and three different shades of Sunburst (Cherry, Sienna and Brown).

• By mid-83, the list was cut down to 4 finishes: Black, Ivory, Sienna and Brown Sunburst.

• In late 1987, the American Standard made its debut with 4 standard (and no custom) finishes: Black, Sunburst, Vintage White and the all-new Gun Metal Blue. Crimson Metallic appeared in mid-88 and Midnight Blue, Midnight Wine and Frost Red in 1989. All these finishes (minus Crimson Metallic dropped after a year) were the stock offering at the end of 1990.

OTHER MODELS

• The first generation of CUSTOM models with a bound body was exclusively offered with a standard 3-tone Sunburst. Some of the early examples, however, look today as if they were sprayed with a 2-tone Sunburst shading owing to the problems experienced by FENDER with the red stain, which often faded away after it was exposed to daylight. When the CUSTOM was revamped in 1972, Sunburst remained the standard finish but by 1975 Black, White, Natural, Walnut and Blond (!) were added to the stock palette. Antigua and Wine (red) were also listed in 1977. Some colours were then phased out (Blond, Walnut, White, Antigua) and prior to its discontinuation in 1981 the model was available with only 4 standard finishes: Black, Natural, Wine and Tobacco Sunburst.

• The THINLINE type I originally came out in 1968 with natural ash and mahogany as its two standard finishes, but Sunburst was quickly added. Shortly after the advent of the THINLINE type II (with humbuckers) mahogany was deleted from the standard finishes and the model was subsequently offered with the same standard finishes as the CUSTOM until its discontinuation in 1979.

• The DELUXE was introduced with at first Walnut as the sole standard finish, but after 1975 it became available with the same palette as the CUSTOM and THINLINE models until its discontinuation in 1981.

• The ELITE Telecaster appeared in 1983 with 6 standard finishes: Black, Natural, Pewter, Artic White, Sienna and Brown Sunburst, not to mention the top-of-the-line WALNUT ELITE. By mid-84 though, all the custom colours previously available at an extra charge became standard during the ELITE 's swan song, i.e. Lake Placid Blue, Candy Apple Red, Aztec Gold, Candy Apple Green, Emerald Green and Wild Cherry as well as the three Stratoburst: Bronze, Black and Blue.

• When FENDER resumed its manufacturing activities after the CBS spin-off, the notion of custom finishes was abandoned and each production model was made available in several standard finishes. The TELE PLUS was introduced in mid-1990 with a selection of 5 standard finishes (Natural, Antique Burst, Ebony Frost, Crimson Frost and Blue Frost) like the newer SET NECK Telecaster (Sapphire Blue Transparent, Autumn Gold, Antique Burst, Crimson Transparent and Ebony Transparent).

Finally, it should be noted that several Telecasters were offered with a unique standard finish which often coined their special designation. For instance: the Mahogany Telecaster in 1963-65, the Paisley Red and Blue Flower models in 1968-69, the Rosewood Telecaster in 1969-72, the Black & Gold Telecaster in 1981-83, the Walnut Elite in 1983-85 and of course the Blond Vintage Reissue since 1981.

CUSTOM FINISHES

Leo Fender always made a point of staying close to musicians, in particular to country and western players, to be perfectly in tune with their needs and requirements. Back in early 50s, some musicians asked for a personalized touch by way of a special finish other than the regular production colour. In other words, they requested a "custom finish."

• The primitive notion of a custom finish was that upon specific request FENDER would paint a guitar in any available colour of the player's choice. At first, this option was the privilege of the artists familiar with the Fullerton factory, but after the mid-50s it made its way into the company's literature. The 1957 catalogue thus specifies: "TELECASTER AND ESQUIRE GUITARS ARE AVAILABLE IN CUSTOM COLOR FINISHES AT AN ADDITIONAL 5% COST." Incidentally, a custom finish is not necessarily a solid colour and in 1957-58 a few Telecasters and Esquires were painted with a *custom* 2-tone Sunburst, otherwise standard on the Stratocaster.

At that time colours were still largely at the customer's discretion, with a possible reference to contemporary car finishes. FENDER was not yet pro-active in offering its own selection of custom finishes, but the company was already using DuPont paints. In the rather conservative environment of the decade, it was fairly outrageous to paint a guitar in red or blue. This explains why original custom-coloured instruments from that period are extremely rare, especially Telecaster guitars.

• In the late 50s, George Fullerton came up with the idea of standardized custom finishes, i.e. specific optional colours which would be offered by FENDER in

Before the Thinline, Fender attempted to lighten the Telecaster via additional routings under the pickguard.

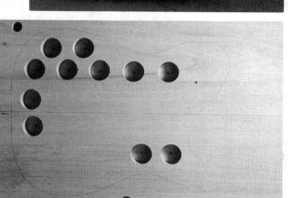

The Set Neck body is made of a core spread of mahogany, drilled with 11 holes of 1.5" to provide a better resonance and save weight.

A run of blond Telecaster bodies drying after being sprayed at the Fullerton factory in the mid-60s. [courtesy John Sprung]

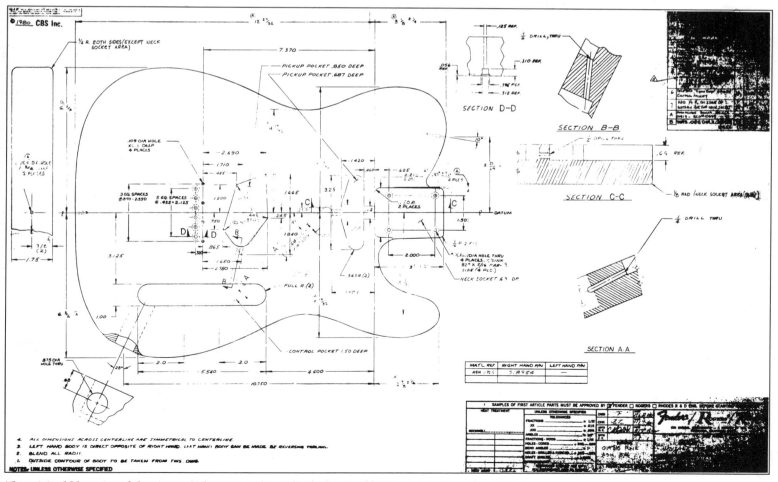

The original blueprint of the Vintage Telecaster as drawn by the late Freddie Tavares in November 1980. [courtesy Fender]

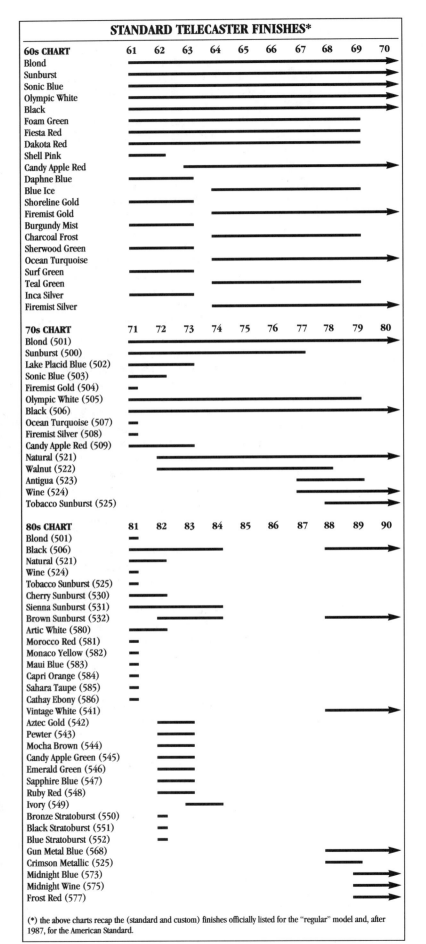

STANDARD TELECASTER FINISHES*

60s CHART — 61 62 63 64 65 66 67 68 69 70
- Blond
- Sunburst
- Sonic Blue
- Olympic White
- Black
- Foam Green
- Fiesta Red
- Dakota Red
- Shell Pink
- Candy Apple Red
- Daphne Blue
- Blue Ice
- Shoreline Gold
- Firemist Gold
- Burgundy Mist
- Charcoal Frost
- Sherwood Green
- Ocean Turquoise
- Surf Green
- Teal Green
- Inca Silver
- Firemist Silver

70s CHART — 71 72 73 74 75 76 77 78 79 80
- Blond (501)
- Sunburst (500)
- Lake Placid Blue (502)
- Sonic Blue (503)
- Firemist Gold (504)
- Olympic White (505)
- Black (506)
- Ocean Turquoise (507)
- Firemist Silver (508)
- Candy Apple Red (509)
- Natural (521)
- Walnut (522)
- Antigua (523)
- Wine (524)
- Tobacco Sunburst (525)

80s CHART — 81 82 83 84 85 86 87 88 89 90
- Blond (501)
- Black (506)
- Natural (521)
- Wine (524)
- Tobacco Sunburst (525)
- Cherry Sunburst (530)
- Sienna Sunburst (531)
- Brown Sunburst (532)
- Artic White (580)
- Morocco Red (581)
- Monaco Yellow (582)
- Maui Blue (583)
- Capri Orange (584)
- Sahara Taupe (585)
- Cathay Ebony (586)
- Vintage White (541)
- Aztec Gold (542)
- Pewter (543)
- Mocha Brown (544)
- Candy Apple Green (545)
- Emerald Green (546)
- Sapphire Blue (547)
- Ruby Red (548)
- Ivory (549)
- Bronze Stratoburst (550)
- Black Stratoburst (551)
- Blue Stratoburst (552)
- Gun Metal Blue (568)
- Crimson Metallic (525)
- Midnight Blue (573)
- Midnight Wine (575)
- Frost Red (577)

(*) the above charts recap the (standard and custom) finishes officially listed for the "regular" model and, after 1987, for the American Standard.

addition to each intrument's standard finish. Based upon the late 50s custom-coloured intruments known to this day, it would appear that Fiesta Red, Shoreline Gold, Lake Placid Blue and Black were among the earliest custom finishes selected by the factory.

By 1961 FENDER released its first "custom chart" featuring 14 finishes displayed in small compressed chips. The colours were: Lake Placid Blue, Daphne Blue, Sonic Blue, Shoreline Gold Metallic, Olympic White, Burgundy Mist Metallic, Black, Sherwood Green Metallic, Foam Green, Surf Green, Inca Silver Metallic, Fiesta Red, Dakota Red and Shell Pink. The chart mentioned "THESE 14 COLORS, PLUS BLOND, AVAILABLE AT 5% ADDITIONAL COST. SUNBURST FINISH STANDARD AT NO EXTRA COST." In the case of Telecaster guitars, Blond was actually available at no extra cost but Sunburst was a chargeable custom finish.

- The first chart also indicated "COLORS SUBJECT TO CHANGE WITHOUT NOTICE" and shortly FENDER began indeed to delete some colours and replace them with other shades. In 1963, the dramatically rare Shell Pink was superseded by Candy Apple Red, which raised to six the number of metallic finishes, then quite trendy. Other changes gradually took place in subsequent charts, but until 1969 FENDER retained 14 optional custom finishes, besides Blond and Sunburst. Most of them were phased out over the 1969-74 period and by 1975 the distinction between standard and custom colours was invalidated. At that time Telecaster guitars could be ordered with only 6 finishes: Blond, Sunburst, Black, White plus Natural (=ash) and Walnut both introduced in 1972.

- True custom finishes were reinstated at the end of 1980 with the inception of the short-lived "international colours" (Ref. 580 through 586 i.e Morocco Red, Monaco Yellow, etc...) available at a $50 additional charge. At the end of 1981 the colour chart was revised to feature a palette of novel finishes, often called the "jewel colours" (Ref. 542 through 548 i.e. Sapphire Blue, Ruby Red, etc...) available at a $75 extra charge. The list was completed in 1982 with three Stratoburst metallic finishes (Bronze, Black, Blue) costing an additional $100 on a Standard Telecaster. Finally, before all production stopped in Fullerton, 75 Telecasters were also released with a limited edition "marble" finish, available in 3 equal batches of different colours (Red, Blue and Gold).

- Since late 1985 several colours, either old or new, have been offered with each Telecaster model but they are available as standard finishes at no extra cost. The "real" custom finishes now come from the Custom Shop established in 1987...as in the old days, a player can request whatever colour he (or she) fancies on a guitar and even more!

For a quick reference, the production finishes used by FENDER on regular Telecasters and Esquires are itemized in chronological charts.

Also worth mentioning:

- The early 50s models finished in Blond (or Blonde as it was initially spelt) are known for their yellowed "butterscotch" colour. Tellies made after 1954 have a "creamier" look, sometimes slightly beige, whilst late 50s guitar feature an "off-white" finish. These different shades basically result from a combination of factors such as the type of lacquer used, the way the finish was applied and to some extent the ageing process.

- On his early guitars, Leo Fender probably used a furniture-grade lacquer, applied with a thin opaqueing colour coat. Contrary to popular belief, though, the early butterscotch colour does not merely result from ageing. Bodies were shot with a tinted lacquer, probably meant to emulate the trendy Blond finish then found on "modern" late 40s furniture. The first prototype built by Leo Fender and George Fullerton in 1949 was sprayed with a white paint, and it is still perfectly white to this day. Leo once indicated that he was originally using an acetate finish on his guitars, and this may well explain the peculiar look of the early Tellies, beyond any cosmetic consideration.

- Although the same basic hue was retained, the finish changed slightly by 1952, approximately at the time FENDER began to order paint supplies from a local company called Spartan Lacquer. Around late 1954 it can be assumed that the

THE **Fender** TELECASTER

factory switched over to more durable automotive finishes, whilst shooting more paint to produce a slightly more opaque Blond shading. Conversely, the appearance of certain 1955-56 guitars suggest that experiments might also have been conducted with different filler pastes and/or undercoats prior to applying the colour coat. At any rate, the ash grain pattern is more visibly showcased on early 50s guitars than on late 50s ones. By 1957, the Blonde finish evolved into the off-white colour it would keep until the early 60s.

- When the '52 reissue project was launched, FENDER engineers (among them Freddie Tavares) reckoned that the paint used in the early 50s was actually white with a touch of beige in it. Ageing mostly made it turn to a yellower shade and to replicate the aged Blonde colour, they ended up mixing a special paint...without too much success!

- The custom finishes offered in the early 60s were DuPont automotive paints usually found on past or current G.M. and Ford cars. In most cases, FENDER kept the paint's automotive namesake and did not bother to coin a specific designation. This explains subtle colour changes in the early charts, such as Firemist Gold ('64 Cadillac colour) vs Shoreline Gold, as FENDER probably modified its own selection in accordance with newer paints used by car manufacturers. These DuPont paints were either enamel lacquers (Duco colours) or Acrylic lacquers (Lucite colours).

- Custom finishes other than those listed in the charts can be found on perfectly original FENDER instruments, e.g. gold sparkle, silver sparkle, purple, aqua marine, blue antigua (a.k.a. "marlin" finish) etc... They were produced in Fullerton either as a "real" custom job for an artist or as a crowd-catcher for a trade show – for instance the Day-glo Telecaster in the colour section – or as part of a a special run for an authorized dealer or simply as an experiment.

- "Ghost finishes" are probably among the rarest of all the exotic unlisted finishes. According to old-timer Alfredo Esquivel from the spray shop, a handful of Telecasters were finished in the mid-60s with a special white paint meant to react under black light and reveal motifs hidden under normal light.

- 60s guitars are not immune from the effects of ageing and, whether Blond or custom-coloured, some of them have ended up today with different shades from those originally applied. A few Sonic Blue guitars turned almond green whilst some Olympic White matured into a yellowed ivory. Some Blonde Tellies also yellowed with age, and in most cases the variation can be traced to the thinness or the absence of a top clear coat to seal the finish properly.

- As implied above, a body usually features three different types of finishing coats: an undercoat (or sealer coat), a colour coat (or opaqueing coat) and a top clear coat. Until 1968, Fender guitars were sprayed with nitro-cellulose lacquers which account for their gently aged and sometimes weathered finish. However, nitro-cellulose lacquers are pretty unstable, harder to deal with and they can generate dangerous toxic fumes. After CBS took over FENDER, polyester finishes were brought in, primarily because they are better suited to mass production. Heavier coats of polyester soon generated a major change in the look and feel of Fender guitars as the company developed its "Thick Skin" high-gloss finish, typical of the 70s instruments. By late 1981, polyurethane replaced polyester for the top coat, and shortly before the close-down of Fullerton it also started to be used for the colour coat.

On the threshold of the 90s, production guitars coming out of the Corona plant are entirely finished with polyurethane, except the Vintage Reissue which has so far retained nitro-cellulose for its colour and top coats. However, the question is how long it will last, as the Environmental Protection Agency (E.P.A.) may disagree with the merits of keeping alive the 50s tradition in a highly pollution-conscious area!

PICKUPS AND WIRINGS

PICKUP SPECIFICATIONS

Overall, Telecaster pickups can be listed in five main categories over the last 40 years.

- ### THE SINGLE COIL BRIDGE PICKUP

This pickup is often considered the heart of the unique Telecaster/Esquire sound. Its construction is fairly rudimentary and consists of a bobbin made of 2 vulcanized fibre plates held together by 6 Alnico magnet slugs and surrounded by a coil. The Alnico magnets (ALNICO = ALuminium-NIckel-CObalt) serve as direct non-adjustable pole pieces. On the early pickups these poles are flush with the top plate of the bobbin, but by late 1955 staggered poles with a raised D and G were introduced to remedy the imbalance in string response. Level-poles reappeared only in 1981 on the '52 Vintage Reissue and were later reinstated on the American Standard.

In the old days, pickups were not wound to an exacting number of turns but primarily engineered to deliver a certain output on a volt-meter with a 20% tolerance. This explains why there are substantial variations in the measurements of older pickups. The earliest bridge units may thus feature more than 10000 turns of wire and a few of them originally boasted a DC resistance well above 9k Ohms. Such a high output is compounded by the fact that Leo Fender did not initially use 42 gauge wire, but slightly skinnier 43 gauge with a higher DC resistance. This particular feature accounts for the powerful twangy singing tone of Broadcasters. The shift to 42 gauge wire took place in the very early 50s, but is fairly difficult to pinpoint more precisely without taking several old pickups apart.

Bridge pickups made during the 50s otherwise feature on average 9200 turns of 42 gauge wire, meant to deliver anything between 7k and 7.8k Ohms prior to installation in the guitar. At any rate, even pickups precisely wound to the same numbers of turns do not necessarily show the very same resistance on a volt-meter! When the old-style hand-winding machines (or rather "hand-guiding" machines) were replaced by automatic winders in the early 60s, FENDER toyed with conversion ratios between the number of turns reading on the counter and the actual number of turns in the pickup. Early CBS blueprints from 1965 indicate that bridge pickups were then wound to 1500 counter turns, meant to equate 7500 actual turns. Ratios were changed back and forth, but on the whole mid-60s and 70s pickups feature an average 7800 actual turns and a resistance ranging between 6k and 6.8k Ohms. In the early 80s, FENDER recaptured some of the old specs thanks to the research carried out for the Vintage Reissue project.

What distinguishes the Tele bridge pickup from other Fender single coil units is the metal back plate under the bobbin. This plate, made of tin until early 1951 and copper-coated theriafter, serves several purposes. It acts as a shield and ground conductor as well as intensifying the magnetic field. Bearing in mind the specific installation of the pickup, electronic shielding was probably the main consideration behind the back plate. It may, however, contribute to unwanted feedback and microphonic noises and this is the reason why FENDER decided to delete it in 1983 on the newer Standard Telecaster. The result is slightly different measurements and performance between the Vintage and the Standard Telecaster lead pickups.

Cosmetically speaking, the first pickups featured a bobbin with two black fibre plates. In 1965 FENDER changed for a light grey bottom plate and after 1968 for a dark grey bottom plate (and also top plate in the late 70s). All black bobbins were reinstated in the early 80s when the copper back plate underneath the bobbin was discarded. Otherwise, prior to winding the coil, the bobbin is dipped in clear lacquer to insulate the magnets from the coil. After the coil is wound, the whole assembly is also immersed in hot wax to saturate the coil. In the mid-60s, some of Leo Fender's tricks-of-the-trade got lost in the CBS text book and the waxing process went amiss. It was therefore suspended for a while and resumed only in the 80s.

- ### THE SINGLE COIL NECK PICKUP

The neck pickup shares the same basic construction as the bridge unit, but it boasts a few specific features. First of all, its bobbin is noticeably smaller and the coil has fewer windings than the bridge unit. Besides, it is encased in a metal shell to protect the coil from electronic interference and therefore its individual

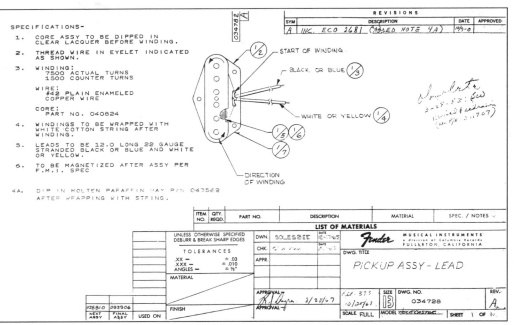

Lead pickup factory blueprint drawn in December 1965. [courtesy Fender]

1950 Broadcaster bridge pickup. Note the tiny notches meant to guide the coil wire to the eyelets. [photo by John Sprung]

Top: mid-50s bridge pickup with flush poles. Middle: late 50s pickup with raised D and A poles. Bottom: late 60s pickup with staggered poles.

Neck pickup factory blueprint drawn in December 1965. At that time, both neck and bridge pickups were wound for the same number of turns. [courtesy Fender]

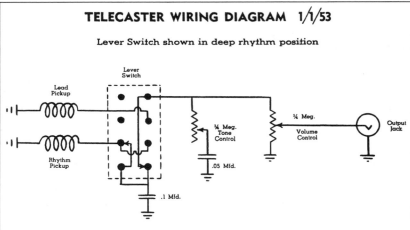

TELECASTER WIRING DIAGRAM 1/1/53

Lever Switch shown in deep rhythm position

Lead Pickup
Rhythm Pickup
Lever Switch
¼ Meg. Tone Control
.05 Mfd.
¼ Meg. Volume Control
Output Jack
.1 Mfd.

The 1953-67 wiring circuit as reproduced in 50s Fender service manual

Disencased 60s neck pickup.

0s bumbucker without shielding cover.

*e 70s bumbucker designed by Seth Lover is fitted with
djustable poles offset in two rows.*

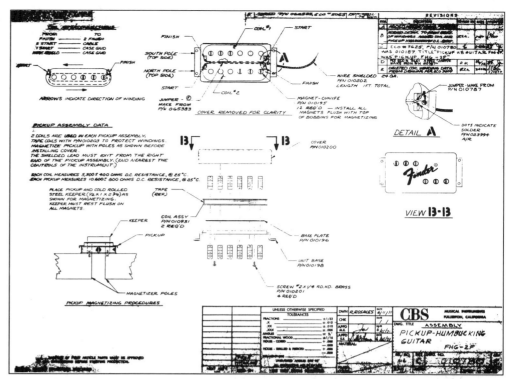

This factory blueprint of Fender's first bumbucker was drawn in June 1971. [courtesy Fender]

*The dual red
Lace Sensor
found on the
Tele Plus is
currently
Fender's
ottest pickup.
[courtesy Fender]*

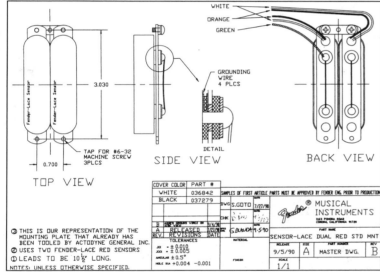

*The Elite
Telecaster
pickup is a
bumbucker
built around
two small
bobbins.*

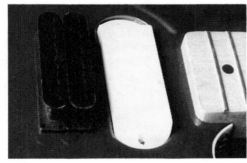

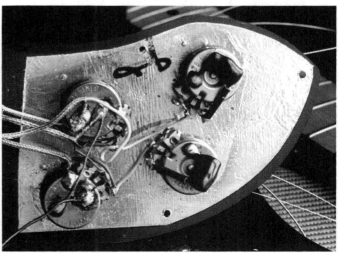

*The Elite's
PC board.*

*Top: Esquire wiring circuit featuring paper capacitors.
Middle: Telecaster wiring featuring ceramic disks.
Bottom: 70s Custom wiring with mylar capacitors.*

BRIDGE PICKUPS SPECIFICATIONS

DATA	1950s early 1960s	late 1960s 1970s	1970s Humbucker	Vintage Reissue	Elite Humbucker	1980s Standard
TYPE OF WIRE	42GA plain enamel	42GA plain enamel then polysol	42GA polysol	42GA plain enamel	42GA polysol	42GA plain enamel
TURNS OF WIRE (average)	9200	7800	10000 both coils	9200	8000 both coils	9200
TYPE OF MAGNET	Alnico 5	Alnico 5	Cunife	Alnico 5	Alnico 2	Alnico 5
DC RESISTANCE (in Ohms)	7500	6400	10600 both coils	7400	11500 both coils	7100
INDUCTANCE (in Henries)	3.21	2.10	4.85	3.58	5.88	3.13
"Q" FACTOR	2.69	2.06	2.87	3.04	3.21	2.77

NECK PICKUP SPECIFICATIONS

DATA	1950s early 1960s	late 1960s 1970s	1970s Humbucker	Vintage Reissue	Elite Humbucker	1980s Standard
TYPE OF WIRE	43GA plain enamel	43GA plain enamel then polysol	42GA polysol	43GA plain enamel	42GA polysol	43GA plain enamel
TURNS OF WIRE (average)	8000	7800	10000 both coils	8000	6000 both coils	8000
TYPE OF MAGNET	Alnico 5	Alnico 5	Cunife	Alnico 5	Alnico 2	Alnico 5
DC RESISTANCE (in Ohms)	7700	6900	10600 both coils	7800	8800 both coils	7500
INDUCTANCE (in Henries)	2.15	2.00	4.85	2.29	3.38	2.20
"Q" FACTOR	1.75	1.82	2.87	1.84	2.41	1.84

LACE SENSOR SPECIFICATIONS

DATA	GOLD	SILVER	BLUE	RED	DUAL RED
DC RESISTANCE (in Ohms)	5800	7100	12800	14500	29500
PEAK FREQUENCY (in Herz)	4300	3300	2200	2000	1700
INDUCTANCE (in Henries)	2.40	3.38	6.58	8.12	16.04
"Q" FACTOR	2.60	2.99	3.23	3.52	3.41

pole pieces are concealed. Judging from the various disencased specimens examined by this author, the neck pickup has always kept level poles, but whilst they were flush with the top (and bottom) plate on the early units, they are slightly protruding at both ends on more recent ones.

From the outset the neck pickup was wound with 43 gauge wire and, unlike the bridge unit, it never changed to 42 gauge wire. Leo Fender was probably satisfied with the sound he was getting from the pickup "as is" and, bearing in mind the size of the bobbin, a coil with 42 gauge windings would have delivered a lower resistance. On the average, neck pickups from the 50s have about 8000 turns of wire and a DC resistance ranging 7.3k and 8.1k Ohms. In the early 60s, the inception of auto-winders and conversion ratios brought about some confusion, and by 1965 CBS documents

indicate that the neck pickup should be wound with 1500 counter turns (=7500 actual turns) exactly as for the bridge pickup. The number of turns changed back and forth in the late 60s before settling down to an average 7800 turns, which gave a resistance of 6.5k to 7.3k Ohms with 43 gauge wire. After 1981, FENDER did its best to retrieve the old specifications, i.e. a resistance ranging between 7.3k and 8.1k Ohms.

- **THE 70s HUMBUCKING PICKUP**

The pickup found on the Deluxe and the second generation of Thinline and Custom models was designed by former Gibson engineer Seth Lover. His Fender brainchild features two coils, each wound with 5000 turns of 42 gauge wire and a resistance of 5300 Ohms +/- 400 Ohms (i.e. a nominal resistance of 10.6k for both coils together).

Whilst adopting the humbucking mode for FENDER, Seth Lover was keen to retain a brighter sound and a higher resonant peak frequency than a Gibson pickup. Besides, the magnets were also to serve as direct adjustable pole pieces (cf the 1953 single coil "Alnico" pickup he designed for Gibson). To this end, Seth used a special alloy made of Copper-Nickel-Ferrite (=Cunife), which was then the only magnetic material likely to be machined and threaded. Cunife magnets also contributed to providing a concentrated flux field and keeping the inductance to a lower level (hence more trebles) than Alnico V, all else being equal.

The 70s Fender humbucker is fitted with 12 threaded magnets but, once the metal cover is soldered, only 6 – split in two offset rows – are fully adjustable in height from the top. It remained in production between 1971 and early 1981 and disappeared from the catalogue with the discontinuation of the Deluxe and Custom models.

- **THE ELITE HUMBUCKING PICKUP**

Although it was not clearly advertised as such in 1983, the pickups engineered for the Elite Telecaster are indeed double coil humbuckers. Besides, unlike the 70s unit, they were produced in two distinct versions for the neck and the bridge positions.

Designed with an active electronics environment in mind, Elite pickups are fitted with weaker Alnico II magnets meant to facilitate the string vibration and improve sustain (less pull). Each pair of black plastic-moulded bobbins is wrapped with 6000 turns (neck) and 8000 turns (bridge) of 42 gauge poly-coated wire and totally encapsulated in a white plastic casing filled with foam resin. The Elite humbuckers do not have adjustable pole pieces and it is generally impossible to tinker with them, without running the risk of completely destroying the coils.

Although it was a sensible attempt to combine the best of two different worlds (i.e. Fender and Gibson), the Elite Telecaster did not make a lasting impact and it was produced only from mid-1983 until late 1984.

- **THE FENDER-LACE SENSORS**

This new generation of "pickups" results from the cooperation between FENDER and a scientist by the name of Don Lace, head of a California-based R&D firm called ACTODYNE GENERAL. Don Lace first approached FENDER in late 1983 to suggest new pickup concepts rooted in his vast experience in the field of magnetic and sensing devices. After the CBS spin-off, talks were resumed in June 1985 and an agreement was eventually signed in September 1986 for the development of a whole range of pickups for guitars and basses. The Strat Plus introduced in early 1987 was the first Fender instrument equipped with the radically innovative "acoustic emission sensors" designed by Don Lace.

The detailed characteristics of the Lace sensors, which are not produced by FENDER but by ACTODYNE, are still classified even for Fender people! Basically, they are passive units built around an intricate array of low energy particle magnets. The conventional pole pieces are thus superseded by 36 micro comb teeth and the inner core of the sensor is framed by metal sides (called Radiant Field Barriers) to eliminate hum and provide quietness of operation. Since 1986, several variants with a distinct tonal response have been developed for electric guitars and are identified by their colour coding:

- Gold = classic late 50s Stratocaster single coil sound
- Blue = clean late 50s humbucker sound
- Silver= punchier Stratocaster sound with more mid-range
- Red = high output humbucker sound

and the hottest of them all, the Dual Red consisting of two Red sensors hooked up in series.

The James Burton model was the first Telecaster to be fitted with a combination of Lace sensors, now also available on the Tele Plus.

For a quick reference, the basic specifications of all these pickups are listed in three separate charts respectively dealing with the bridge pickups, the neck pickups and the Fender-Lace sensors. The featured data come either from factory files, including the information researched by Dan Smith and John Page while preparing the vintage reissue models, or were specially gathered for this author by Fender electronic engineer Rick Rodriguez, who kindly helped with the measurement of more recent pickups.

Regarding older bridge and neck pickups, the charts reproduce the average specifications of only two generations, which loosely speaking refer to the pre-CBS and the CBS eras. *Substantial variations may indeed occur in the measurements of older pickups, even for units of the same vintage.* Besides, such measurements may not indicate the actual readings of these pickups when brand new because of the likely effects of the ageing process. Last but not least, the pickups were all measured on a stand-alone basis, prior to installation in a guitar, with the controls bypassed and without taking into account the capacitance of a typical cord.

Now, a few words of explanation concerning the main parameters listed in the charts.

• the RESISTANCE represents the restriction opposed to the flow of electricity because of the wire gauge and length (= number of turns). As a quick rule of thumb, the lower the resistance (all else being equal) the weaker the output and the clearer the tone. Regarding Telecaster pickups, a 43 gauge wire is skinnier than a 42 gauge wire, hence a higher resistance for an equal number of windings.

• the INDUCTANCE measures the resistance to alternating curents in relation to the magnetic field. Basically, the higher the inductance, the greater the output but also the greater the loss of high end.

• the "Q" FACTOR is supposed to rate the efficiency of a coil and is largely an expression of the ratio of inductance to resistance. A pickup with a higher "Q" (all else being equal) would emphasize a narrower band of frequencies and conversely a pickup with a lower "Q" would emphasize a larger band of frequencies. For the sake of comparison, all the Q factors listed in the charts have been calculated as per the following formula: $Q = 2\pi\ FL : R$
where $2\pi = 6.28$
F = a constant frequency of 1000hz
L = the inductance in Henries
R = the resistance in Ohms

PICKUP ASSEMBLIES

STANDARD DUAL PICKUP ASSEMBLY

Three distinct configurations have been successively used by FENDER since 1950.

1950 - 1952

The original wiring found on the 2-pu Esquire, Broadcaster,"No-Caster" and early Telecaster is characterized by the absence of a "real" tone control and the 3-way selector switch offers the following combinations (F= forward, M=middle, R= rear):
F = neck pickup alone with a pre-set bassy sound and no tone control
M = neck pickup alone with a natural sound and no tone control
R = both pickups together with the neck pickup "blended" into the bridge pickup according to the setting of the 2nd ("tone") control

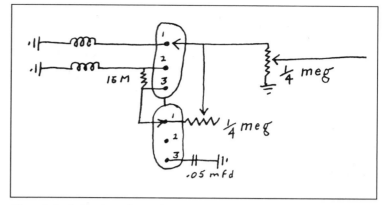

The original circuit as drawn by Leo Fender himself. [courtesy Richard Smith]

In other words, the 2nd control operates as a blender or pan control between the 2 pickups when the selector switch is in the rear position. Besides, it has no effect whatsoever in the other two positions. Electronically speaking, this assembly features:
• two 250K Ohm audio potentiometers for the controls
• one .05 MFD capacitor connected between the switch and the master volume pot
• one 15K Ohm resistor soldered on the CRL switch.

1953 - 1967

In 1952 the assembly was modified by Leo Fender to incorporate a real tone control, but in doing so Leo discarded any two pickup combination. The post-52 wiring thus provides the following settings:
F = neck pickup alone with a pre-set bassy sound but no tone control
M = neck pickup alone with proper tone control
R = bridge pickup alone with proper tone control

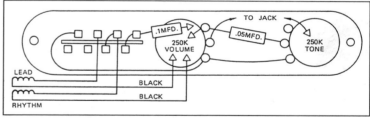

1953-1967 circuit.

Electronically speaking, this second variant features:

• two 250K Ohm audio pots for the controls

• one .05 MFD capacitor connected between the 2 pots

• one .1 MFD capacitor connected between the CRL switch and the master volume pot but it no longer incorporates a 15K resistor soldered on the selector switch.

AFTER 1967

The wiring was finally modified in late 1967 to provide a more traditional 2-pickup switching, i.e.:
F = neck pickup alone with tone control
M = both pickups together with tone control
R = bridge pickup alone with tone control

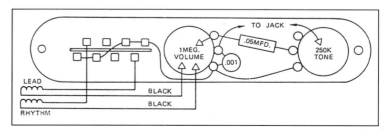

Post-67 circuit.

The third variant finally did away with the pre-set bassy sound obtained in the neck position since 1950. This feature is often overlooked simply because many players clipped off the .1 MFD capacitor connected between the switch and the volume pot on pre-68 guitars. Others completely rewired the assembly to obtain a classic 2-pickup switching.

Electronically speaking, the newer wiring initially featured:

- two 250K Ohm audio pots for the controls

- one .05 MFD capacitor connected between the 2 pots

- one .001 MFD capacitor soldered on the volume pot for added brilliance at lower settings. But, in 1969, the 250K pots were gradually superseded by 1 MEG units, bearing in mind that a 250K pot gives a smoother taper but less highs than a 1 MEG pot, which otherwise has more roll-off. However, by late 1981 the tone pot reverted to 250K instead of 1 MEG and in 1983 the tone capacitor was changed for a less bassy .022 MFD. In late 1987, the American Standard came out with a modified circuitry featuring a TBX tone control, first introduced in 1983 on the Elite Telecaster (see below: other assemblies). The TBX control features a dual concentric pot (250K audio/1 MEG linear), one .022 MFD capacitor and a 82K resistor. At the same time, the volume pot reverted to 250K instead of the 1 MEG value in use since 1969.

The Vintage Telecaster is factory-equipped with a 1952-67 type assembly, but it is furnished with an electronic parts kit meant to update the guitar to post-67 specifications.

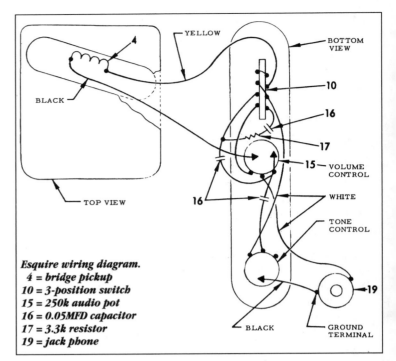

Esquire wiring diagram.
 4 = bridge pickup
10 = 3-position switch
15 = 250k audio pot
16 = 0.05MFD capacitor
17 = 3.3k resistor
19 = jack phone

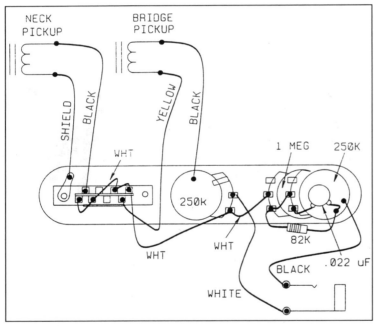

American Standard circuit with TBX tone control.

SINGLE PICKUP ASSEMBLY

The single pickup assembly associated with the ESQUIRE is essentially a Telecaster circuit minus the neck pickup. Unlike other single pickup guitars (e.g. Les Paul Junior) usually equipped with a single volume and tone control, the Esquire was fitted with a 3-way switch meant to provide different tonal responses. The settings work as follows:

- F = the pickup is wired through two capacitors and one resistor to offer a pre-set bassy sound with no tone control

- M = the pickup is normally wired through volume and tone controls

- R = the pickup is directly wired to the output jack to give a hotter lead sound with no tone control.

The 2nd control operates only in the middle position but it works as a real tone control. The rationale behind this peculiar wiring used until 1969 was to give to the single pickup Esquire tone possibilities similar to those of a dual pickup guitar. Electronically speaking, this assembly features:

- two 250K Ohm audio pots for the controls

- three .05 MFD capacitors

- one 2.5K resistor, later replaced by a 3.3K resistor after the mid-50s.

OTHER PICKUP ASSEMBLIES

- THINLINE (TYPE II)

The Thinline was originally fitted with a post-67 standard dual-pickup assembly. In late 1971, the model was revamped with two humbuckers but kept the same controls arrangement, i.e. master volume and tone controls plus a 3-way position switch. However, the advent of humbuckers entailed a change in the value of the pots (250K instead of 1 MEG) and tone capacitor (.022 MFD instead of .05 MFD). Besides, the .001 MFD capacitor added in late 1967 to the volume control of the standard assembly was also discarded.

- CUSTOM (TYPE II)

The original Custom model shared the same electronics as the regular Telecaster. The Custom type II introduced in 1972 is characterized by a humbucker in the neck position and a 4-control assembly, with separate volume and tone settings for each pickup. The new Custom kept 1 MEG pots but, as on the Thinline type II, .022 MFD capacitors were adopted for the tone controls.

- DELUXE

Electronically speaking, the Deluxe could be described as a cross between the revamped Thinline and Custom models introduced at the same period of time. It sports two humbuckers, a 4-control assembly and a 3-way toggle switch, that is a configuration closely resembling a Gibson guitar! Otherwise, the Deluxe is fitted with the same harness as the Custom, i.e. four 1 MEG pots with one .022 MFD capacitor on each tone control.

- ELITE

Built around active electronics, the Elite assembly features two specially designed humbucking pickups, four controls, a 3-way toggle switch and a PC board crammed with components. Each pickup has a separate volume control (1 MEG audio pot), but the guitar has a unique tone circuit consisting of one TBX control (closer to the jack output) and one MDX control (closer to the bridge).

This circuit works as follows:

- the TBX is a high-range control with a centre detent that gives the standard Fender sound. Rotating the knob clockwise from its mid-point click-stop position enhances the higher resonant peak of the pickups. Rotating it counterclockwise cuts off high frequencies.

- the MDX is a mid-range control which gives a variable boost of up to 6db while cutting off high frequencies.

Electronically, the TBX features a dual concentric pot (250K audio/1 MEG linear) with a .022 MFD capacitor and a 82K resistor, whilst the MDX uses a 50K linear pot. The built-in PC board comprises no less than 4 transistors, 12 capacitors and 17 resistors and is powered by a 9-volt battery. The output jack acts as a on/off switch for the circuitry so that there is no drain on the battery when the guitar is unplugged.

- JAMES BURTON

The Burton is fitted with 3 different Lace sensors: Blue in the neck position, Silver in the middle and Red near the bridge. They are wired to a 5-way selector switch which allows for the following combinations:

1. neck pickup alone
2. neck and middle pickup together
3. neck and bridge pickup together in parallel
4. bridge and middle pickup together
5. bridge pickup alone.

Otherwise, the assembly features a master volume and tone controls with 250k audio pots and one .022 MFD capacitor.

- ALBERT COLLINS

The Collins has a 60s style standard dual-pickup assembly, except that the single coil neck pickup is replaced by a DiMarzio humbucker. Otherwise, the circuit features two 250k pots with one .05 MFD capacitor for tone.

- DANNY GATTON

The Gatton is equipped with special pickups made by Joe Barden in Virginia. These pickups are side-by-side humbuckers which fit in the same space as regular single coil pickups. Otherwise, the model features a standard dual-pickup assembly with a 500k pot for the master volume.

- TELE PLUS

The newer Plus features a Blue Lace sensor in the neck position and a dual Red in the bridge position. Besides a classic 3-way switching, the model is also fitted with mini toggle switch acting as a splitter for the dual Red sensor. Otherwise, the tone control is of the TBX type like American Standard.

- SET NECK TELECASTER

The latest brainchild from the Custom Shop is available with either a 2-pickup or a 3-pickup assembly. The dual pickup models are fitted with two DiMarzio humbuckers, a classic 3-way pickup switching and a coil-splitting mini toggle switch. The 3-pickup model has an additional single coil unit (Stratocaster type) in the middle position and a 5-way selector switch. Both variants are fitted with a master volume (250K audio pot) and a TBX tone control.

On a more general note, the following points are worth mentioning about Fender pickup assemblies.

- Until the early 80s, FENDER used the same type of spring-loaded selector switch, branded "CRL 1452." The early 50s units usually feature 2 patent numbers (PAT 2,291,516 and 2,291,517), but a third patent number (2,503,885) is also mentioned after the mid-50s. During the 60s, the first two patent numbers were deleted and only the third one remained stamped on the chassis. Over the last few years, FENDER has primarily used replicas of the original CRL 1452 switch.

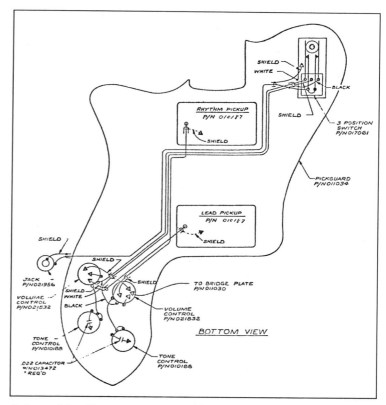

Deluxe wiring diagram.

- Until the late 60s, Fender exclusively used waxed cotton insulated wires (a.k.a. "cloth wires") on all its pickup assemblies. Beginning in 1968, they were gradually replaced by plastic-coated wires. Cloth wires were later resurrected for the '52 Vintage Reissue although the earliest samples were actually fitted with plastic wires.

- The early 50s wirings are characterized by a bright-coloured sheath covering the cloth wires alongside the selector switch.

- After the late 70s, pickup leads are usually housed in pairs inside a flexible white plastic tube.

- Beginning in 1983 a metal-braided sheath was first used to shield the wires coming out of the neck pickup.

- On the 70s guitars with humbuckers, pickups leads are shielded braided wires of the Gibson-type and not plastic-coated wires.

- On the regular dual and single pickup assemblies, the wires are colour-coded: black/yellow for the bridge p.u. and black/white for the neck p.u. and the jack output wires. Exceptions do exist though, particularly on mid-60s guitars which may come with blue/yellow or green/yellow wires.

- The coil of the bridge pickup was at first protected by black tape, but after 1952 FENDER switched over to black (briefly) and then white cotton string. The finished coils were dipped in molten paraffin wax until the mid-60s and today the white string is often darkened with dust and dirt on older pickups. It is much cleaner on late 60s pickups, which were not dipped in paraffin wax. Since the early 70s, the colour of the cotton string has reverted to black whilst the wax-dipping procedure has also been resumed in the early 1980s.

- Between 1950 and 1961, pickup assemblies featured white paper capacitors, either flat or cylindrical, on which the value and specs are written in black/blue lettering (e.g. "ZYW 1S5 - .05MFD" or "ZNW 1P1 - .1MFD"). Up to the mid-50s, the paper capacitors were often waxed.

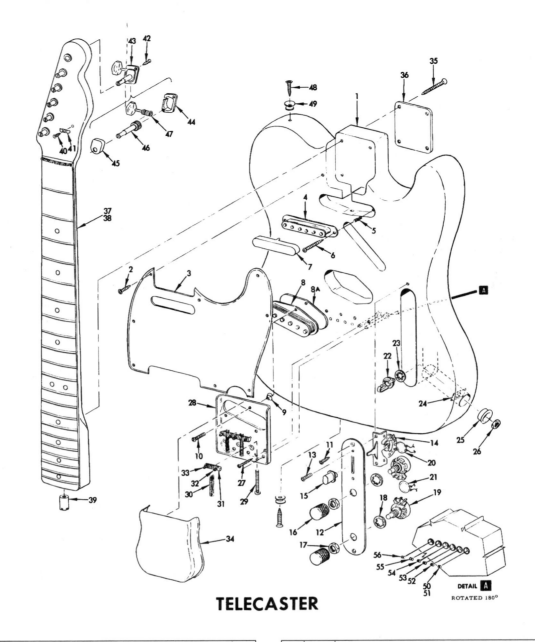

TELECASTER

DRAWING KEY NUMBER	PART NUMBER	PART DESCRIPTION	QUANTITY REQUIRED PER ASSY
		BODY ASSEMBLY	
1	040782	Body - Sunburst	1
		PICKGUARD ASSEMBLY	
2	015578	Screw - SM. OV. HD. PHIL. #4 x 1/2 STL. NKL. PLT.	8
3	070698	Pickguard White, Black White	1
		PICKUP ASSEMBLY, RHYTHM	
4	034736	Magnetic Pickup Assembly (Rhythm)	1
5	019232	Spring	2
6	016295	Screw - WOOD. RD. HD. PHIL. #3 x 1 STL. NKL. PLT.	2
7	033027	Cover - Pickup	1
		PICKUP ASSEMBLY, LEAD	
8	034728	Magnetic Pickup Assembly (Lead)	1
8A	010371	Elevation Plate	1
9	019240	Spring - Compression, 4 coils, 3/8 F. L.	3
10	015826	Screw - MACH. RD. HD. PHIL. #6 - 32 x 1/4 STL. NKL. PLT.	3
		MASTER CONTROL	
11	015578	Screw - SM. OV. HD. PHIL. #4 x 1/2 STL. NKL. PLT.	2
12	033134	Plate - Master Control	1
13	022186	Screw - MACH. PH. HD. PHIL. #6 - 32 x 3/8 STL. NKL. PLT.	2
14	017053	Switch - 3 position	1
15	019448	Knob - Switch	1
16	013359	Knob - Control	2
17	016352	Nut - Hex 3/8 x 32 THD.	2
18	016436	Washer - Lock, Internal Tooth 3/8	2
19	032367	Control - Volume and Tone, 250K Audio	2
20	015537	Capacitor 0.1 MFD. 50V, 10%	1
21	015552	Capacitor 0.05 MFD. 50V, 20%	1
		OUTPUT ASSEMBLY	
22	021956	Jack - Phone, 2 cond. Open Circuit	1
23	016436	Washer - Lock, Internal Tooth 3/8	1
24	010355	Retainer	1
25	010363	Plate	1
26	016352	Nut - Hex 3/8 x 32 THD.	1
		ADJUSTABLE BRIDGE ASSEMBLY	
27	016188	Screw - WOOD. OV. HD. PHIL. 6 x 1 STL. NKL. PLT.	4
28	010330	Plate - Base	1
29	015834	Screw - MACH. RD. HD. PHIL. 6/32 x 1.1/4 STL. NKL. PLT.	3
30	018689	Spring - Compression	3
31	013151	Bar - Adjustable Bridge	3
32	016113	Screw - SET. Hd. less Slotted 6-32 x 5/16 STL. NKL. PLT.	2
33	016105	Screw - SET. Hd. less Slotted 6-32 x 7/16 STL. NKL. PLT.	4
34	027706	Cover - Bridge	1

DRAWING KEY NUMBER	PART NUMBER	PART DESCRIPTION	QUANTITY REQUIRED PER ASSY
		NECK AND KEY ASSEMBLY	
35	015644	Screw - WOOD. OV. HD. PHIL. #8 x 2 STL. NKL. PLT.	4
36	010215	Plate - Neck	1
37	040881	Neck and Key Assembly - includes, neck with decals keys installed, adjusting nut. No string guide included.	1
38	040899	Neck Fabrication Assembly - No Keys included, adjusting nut and decal included.	1
39	012252	Nut - Neck Rod Adjusting	
		STRING GUIDE ASSEMBLY	
40	016329	Screw - WOOD. RD. HD. PHIL. #3 x 3/8, STL. NKL. PLT.	1
41	010389	Guide - String	1
		KEY ASSEMBLY	
42	016329	Screw - WOOD. RD. HD. PHIL. #3/8 STL. NKL. PLT.	12
43	053694	Key Assembly Complete (Fender Metal)	6
44	033738	Cover - Key Assembly	6
45	033761	Housing - Key Assembly	6
46	034330	Post and Gear Assembly	6
47	034363	Head and Worm Assembly	6
		STRAP BUTTON ASSEMBLY	
48	016188	Screw - WOOD. OV. HD. PHIL. #6 x 1 STL. NKL. PLT.	2
49	012344	Button - Neck Strap	2
		STRING ASSEMBLY	
50	017798	String Set Complete (6 Strings) (1500)	1
51	017806	"E" String (1) (1501)	1
52	017814	"B" String (2) (1502)	1
53	017822	"G" String (3) (1503)	1
54	017830	"D" String (4) (1504)	1
55	017848	"A" String (5) (1505)	1
56	017855	"E" String (6) (1506)	1
		MISCELLANEOUS PARTS (Not Illustrated)	
	017103	Strap - Guitar	1
	045237	Manual - Instruction	1

- Beginning in 1961, paper capacitors were superseded by ceramic disks, of specific colours (i.e. yellow, red, orange) according to the electronic value and the period of issue.

- With the introduction of lower value capacitors (.022 MFD) on the guitars with humbuckers in the early 70s, FENDER first used mylar capacitors (initially coloured in dark blue) instead of ceramic disks. The latter remained, however, in use on single coil pickup assemblies throughout the 70s.

- Mixed assemblies with one ceramic and one mylar capacitor are first found in the early 80s on both Standard and Vintage Telecasters. Mylar capacitors are identified by their oblong shape and (usually) orange colour.

HARDWARE

TUNING KEYS

- From 1950 up to 1967 Telecaster guitars were fitted with keys made by Chicago-based company, KLUSON MANUFACTURING CO. These tuners are characterized by their split shaft with a well for the string end and their oval-shaped metal button. However, during that period, four slightly different types of shells can be distinguished.

  - on the guitars made until mid-1951, the shell is stamped with the words "KLUSON DELUXE" on the back and "PAT.APPLD" on one side, whilst the bottom base shows a "2356766 PAT.APPLD" marking. Besides, the early Kluson tuners feature a closed shell, without a protruding shaft.

  - the keys found on the guitars made between mid-51 and 1957 do not feature any brand stamp on the outer shell, but are usually stamped with "2356766 PAT.APPLD" on the bottom base.

  - by 1957 the keys were again stamped with "KLUSON DELUXE" in a single line whilst the bottom base read "PATENT NO D-169400."

  - the latest version which appeared in 1964 has the words "KLUSON DELUXE" stamped separately in two lines on the back-shell and "PATENT N0 D-164900" on the bottom base.

- In the course of 1967, Kluson tuners were gradually phased out and replaced by Fender-designed keys, characterized by an octagonal button shape and the backwards "F" for Fender stamped on the back-shell. Although designed in Fullerton, these keys were manufactured by SCHALLER and the gear inside the shell is thus stamped with "MADE IN W. GERMANY." This type of key remained in use on most Telecaster guitars until 1983.

- In 1973, the Deluxe came out with one-piece die-cast Deluxe Schaller keys, characterized by the lack of split shaft and a Fender logo stamped on the back. A slightly different version of Deluxe Schaller keys was later adopted by the Elite and Standard Telecasters released in 1983, with a pearloid button on the Walnut and Gold Elite models.

- As the KLUSON company went out of business, the Vintage Telecaster is equipped with Kluson-style replicas made by the GOTOH company in Japan. Otherwise, the current production models display improved die-cast Schaller keys. Mechanically they are probably better tuners than the early Kluson heads, but conceptually they miss the practical split shaft with a well for the string end!

HEADSTOCK STRING GUIDE

- The earliest 1950 models were initially deprived of any string guide, but very soon a round string guide was added on the headstock to press down the E and B strings. This round guide is screwed on somewhere near the D and G-string tuning posts and can be found in this position on guitars made until about mid-56.

- In 1956, Fender changed for a "butterfly" retainer which at first kept the same location as the early 50s round guide. After 1956, however, it was relocated closer to the nut so as to be in the alignment of the A-string tuning post.

- In early 1972, a second retainer appeared for the G and D strings and it was positioned slightly closer to the nut than the clip holding the E and B strings.

- In mid-83, Fender introduced its newly designed "Ezy-Glider" string tree on the Elite Telecaster. This is still a current feature on production Telecasters but, with the advent of the American Standard, Fender has reverted to only one guide for the E and B strings instead of two. The only exceptions are the Vintage Reissue, fitted with an old-style round guide, and the Deluxe Tele Plus which has no string guide at all because of its special Wilkinson roller nut.

BRIDGE ASSEMBLY

The original bridge assembly featured in the patent filed by Leo Fender in January 1950 was used until mid-83 on all the models fitted with a rear single coil pickup. The only notable exceptions are the guitars equipped with a Bigsby vibrato tailpiece. For the sake of nitty gritty, there are a few details likely to distinguish various types of bridge assemblies.

THE SADDLES

- The earliest 1950 models are fitted with 3 steel saddles ground flat on the bottom, whilst the Broadcasters released by Fall 1950 usually have brass saddles.

- In late 1954 brass saddles were superseded by steel saddles, albeit not ground flat on the bottom and of a slightly smaller diameter than the 1950 sections.

- After mid-58 steel saddles were in turn replaced by threaded saddles, which remained the basic trim until early 1968.

- Beginning in 1968, threaded saddles were phased out in favour of steel saddles featuring a groove for each string. The latter type was kept as a standard appointment until 1983, but in the mid-70s a bridge with 6 individual steel saddles was first fitted to the Custom type II and then offered as an accessory to retrofit other Telecaster guitars.

THE BASE PLATE

- The plates found on the guitars made until late 1954 feature the instrument's serial number stamped below the words "FENDER PAT. PEND."

- After late 1954, the serial number was relocated on the neck plate and the plate was simply stamped with "FENDER PAT. PEND."

- Beginning in 1962, the plate was stamped with "FENDER PAT.NO. DES 164227 2,573,254." These markings were kept until 1983, except on the 70s six-piece bridge which displayed only a "FENDER" brand-stamp without any patent indication.

THE SNAP-ON COVER

Although it often ended as a portable ash tray, the snap-on cover was maintained until mid-1983 on guitars fitted with the original style bridge assembly. The early 50s units display a distinctive solder drop (or at least its mark) on the inner face. This detail comes from the fact that in the old days a wire was soldered to the cover as a contact for electro-plating. Later bridge covers were snapped on racks with spring clips for plating, which explains why they do not have a solder drop on the inner face.

Also worth mentioning:

- In 1953 the two outer brass saddles were notched to allow for a lower adjustment of both E strings.

- In late 1958 the string-through-body pattern was suspended and replaced for about a year by a top-loading system. On "top loader" guitars, the 6 string holes are drilled in the back ridge (and not in the flat base) of the bridge plate. However, when FENDER reverted to the original string-through-body loading, the existing inventory of top loader bridge plates was re-drilled with 6 string holes in the flat base. As a result, late 1959 and 1960 guitars usually come with a bridge plate drilled for both loading patterns.

- the Bigsby vibrato tailpiece was first listed as an option in 1967, but earlier factory-fitted units are known to exist. Guitars with a Bigsby tailpiece feature a 6-piece bridge with threaded saddles and a base plate without any marking.

- the Vintage Reissue model is naturally fitted with a replica of the 1952 bridge assembly, but to avoid any confusion (and forgery!) a small dot is stamped on the base plate under the serial number.

In 1983 the original bridge assembly was phased out (except on the Vintage Reissue model) with the inception of the Elite and (revised) Standard Telecasters.

- The Elite models have a die-cast bridge made by Schaller and characterized by a massive ridge stamped with a backwards "F." Designed for "drop in" string loading (=top loading), it also features 6 asymmetric elongated saddles resting on staggered tracks.

- The 1983 Standard bridge is somewhat reminiscent of the original design, but it features a longer and thicker chrome-plated brass plate without any side ridges. Like the contemporary Elite unit, it is designed for top loading and fitted with 6 asymmetric elongated saddles.

However, the top loading pattern did not prove that popular and FENDER went back to back loading on the American Standard introduced in late 1987. The bridge assembly was also redesigned to incorporate six high density stainless saddles (or "compressed steel" saddles) already developped for the American Standard Stratocaster. To accomodate these new saddles, the string holes have been moved forward in the base plate, ahead of the 3 screws fastening the whole bridge assembly to the body. Incidentally, while the new bridge was being perfected, the first 100 or so American Standard Telecasters were released with 70s style 6-piece bridge.

Other types of bridge assembly were also featured on specific Telecaster models.

- The Thinline type II (with humbuckers) was fitted with the 6-piece bridge of the non-tremolo Stratocaster (with appropriate snap-on bridge cover).

- The Deluxe also sported a Strat-style 6-piece bridge with snap-on cover, albeit with slightly different saddles. In the mid-70s a few Deluxes were also mounted with a complete Stratocaster tremolo bridge assembly.

- The Black and Gold Telecaster came out with a specially designed gold plated 6-piece assembly, made of brass and characterized by a massive ridge with a "FENDER USA" brand stamp.

- The more recent Deluxe Tele Plus is fitted with the tremolo bridge assembly of the American Standard Stratocaster.

PICKGUARD

- Up until late 1954, the standard trim was a one-ply black pickguard, first made of fibre material and then of bakelite, and fastened to the body with 5 screws. The very early black guards were simply buffed after being cut, but it was soon decided to lacquer them for a glossier look. This also explains why the early 50s black guards usually display a visible 5" ring on the underside, as they were probably put on a paint can while being sprayed.

- Although a very few samples are known to exist on early 50s models, it was not until late 1954 that one ply white pickguards became the standard trim on Telecaster guitars.

- In mid-59, the Custom versions were introduced with a 3-ply white pickguard (W/B/W) made of celluloid, often called "nitrate guard" or "green guard" because of their greyish/greenish tint even when brand new. The earliest 3-ply guards were still fastened by 5 screws, but by Summer 1959 all Telecaster pickguards were changed to an 8-screw mount, whether one-ply or 3-ply.

- By the end of 1963, the regular models were also fitted with a 3-ply celluloid guard. However, due to security constraints on the factory premises, these (highly inflammable) nitrate pickguards were discontinued after 1964 and replaced by straight plastic units.

- 1968 saw the introduction of the Thinline model (type I) and its elongated pickguard with a pearloid top face. Some early Thinlines were produced with a straight 3-ply white guard, but most of them have what the Fender afficionados call a "mother-of-toilet-seat" top face! The pickguard shape was redesigned on the Thinline type II and straight 3-ply white guards became the norm whilst pearloid guards were gradually phased out. Oddly enough, it is not unusual to find a pearloid face as the *underside* of some early 70s white pickguards.

- The Deluxe and the Custom type II came out in the early 70s with 3-ply black pickguards (B/W/B) of a specific elongated shape, covering a fair amount of the body face. By 1976 the regular Telecaster as well as the Thinline type II were also fitted with 3-ply black pickguards.

- In the course of 1981, a 3-ply white plastic guard was reinstated on the regular Telecaster,but the Black & Gold Telecaster (logically) retained a 3-ply black pickguard. Likewise, the '52 Vintage Reissue was introduced with a one-ply black guard fastened to the body with only 5 screws.

- In mid-83, the newly designated Standard model changed for a single-ply white guard, initially mounted with 8 screws but soon came down to 5 screws on most production models. Meanwhile, the Elite came out with a 3-ply wing-shaped adhesive-backed separate pickguard, intended to be installed at the owner's discretion.

- Recent models like the American Standard or the Tele Plus reverted to 3-ply white guards mounted with 8 screws, whilst the James Burton or the Set Neck Telecasters are simply left without any pickguard at all. Lastly, it should be noted that the 40th Anniversary model has been released with a unique ivoroid single ply guard matching the binding of the guitar.

OTHER PARTS

- THE KNOBS

With the exception of a few specific models, Telecaster guitars have been consistently fitted with metal knobs, devoid of any numbers or markings. Although they may all look the same to the layman, it would take a few paragraphs to accurately describe the minute details which help distinguish them over the years. Suffice it to say that up to 1956, Fender used heavier "dome" knobs made of brass and thereafter much lighter "flat top" knobs (except on the Vintage Reissue and Set Neck Telecasters). But, this sweeping statement needs additional comments to do justice to the different types of "dome" knobs and "flat" knobs used by FENDER.

For instance:

- The knobs from 1950 and early 1951 are taller and feature a fainter dome as well as a coarser side knurl. Later knobs are not as tall and display a neater dome, but between 1951 and 1956 different types of dome profile and knurl pattern can be distinguished.

- According to the years, "flat" knobs may differ slightly in overall height or in the way the flatted top end blends into the side knurl. Certain 60s knobs have a gently curved top edge descending into the knurl, whilst some 80s knobs have a knurl perfectly flush with a sharp top edge. Likewise, some 70s knobs feature a more prominent bottom lip than late 50s units etc... For the amateur of nitty-gritty, the pictures featured in this book may contribute to opening new vistas on Telecaster knobs!

Otherwise, a few models were also fitted with knobs of a different style.

- The 70s Deluxe and Custom type II initially sported Gibson-style black plastic knobs, with a 1-10 graduation and a metal cap reading VOL. and TONE.

- After 1975, these two models as well as the Thinline type II were fitted with Stratocaster-style black knobs.

- The short lived Elite came out with special white plastic knobs, featuring a serrated rubber insert, a 1-10 graduation and a backward "F" embossed on the top end.

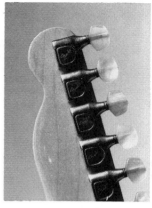

Single line Klusons, no brand.

Single line branded Klusons.

Dual line Klusons.

Late 60s Fender keys.

80s Fender keys with pearloid buttons.

1950 Kluson tuners with "Pat. Appld For" marking stamped on the outer shell. [photo by John Sprung]

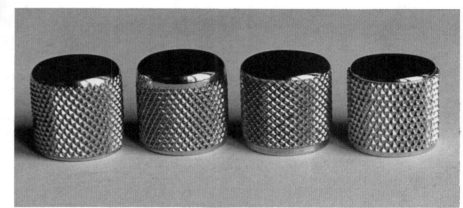

Top: 50s dome knobs (left to right 1950-51-53-55) Bottom: flat knobs (left to right 1958-65-68-75).

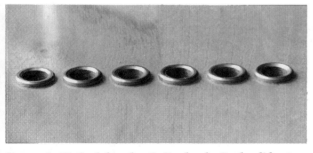

Top: early 50s back ferrules. Quite clearly, Fender did not use a jig to simultaneously drill the 6 string holes. Middle: flush ferrules. Bottom: protruding ferrules.

50s black guards usually feature a 5" ring on the underside.

Top: early 50s milled jack cup. Bottom: jack cup made of pressed steel.

Early 50s bridge with brass saddles.

Mid-50s bridge with steel saddles.

Late 50s bridge with threaded saddles.

Late 60s bridge with grooved steel saddle

Strat-style Thinline II bridge.

1970's six-way bridge.

1983 Standard bridge with Elite saddles.

American Standard bridge.

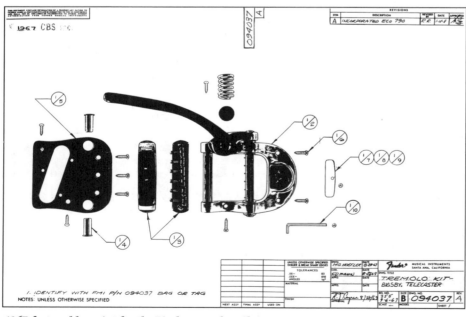

1967 factory blueprint for the Bigsby tremolo tailpiece. [courtesy Fender]

Late 50s top loading bridge [photo by John Sprung]

1953 Telecaster equipped with a fixed-arm Bigsby tailpiece. [photo by Vince Cunetto]

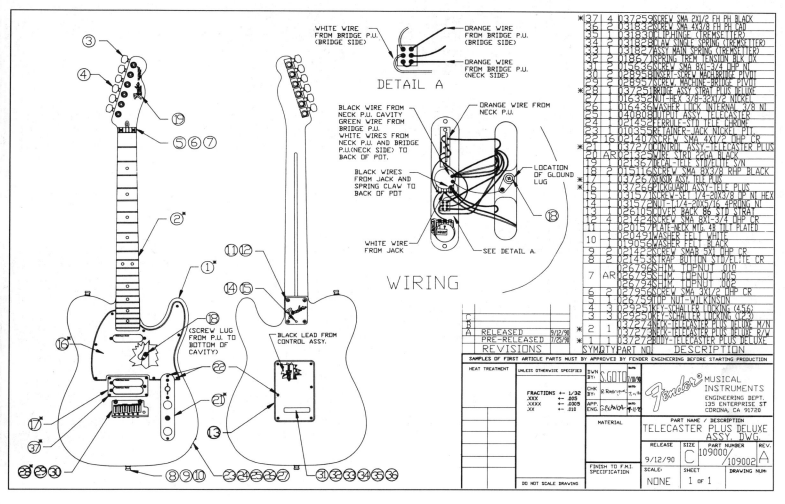

• THE SWITCH TIP

The models produced between 1950 and mid-1956 have a small barrel-like tip on the selector switch. In the 50s these black tips were made by a Chicago-based company by the name of Harry Davies Co. But, the markings underneath read "DAKA WARE" with a patent pending indication on the earlier units and a patent number (2,189,845) on the later ones.

In the course of 1956, the small barrel was replaced by a bigger "top-hat" switch tip, also branded "DAKA WARE" with a patent number. The top hat tip lost its Daka-Ware branding in the course of the 70s, but it remained a standard feature of most Telecaster guitars until 1985, with the following exceptions:

- the 70s Deluxe and Custom models fitted with a Gibson-style toggle switch with matching screwed-on tip
- the Black & Gold model fitted with a Strat-style brass tip
- the Vintage Reissue logically equipped with an early 50s barrel type switch (but not a Daka Ware!).
- the Elite Telecaster also mounted with a Gibson-style toggle switch.

On the American Standard and the subsequent production models introduced since 1987, Fender has reverted to the original style barrel switch tip. The only exception so far is the Set Neck Telecaster mounted with a Strat-style metal tip.

• THE JACK CUP

The earliest Telecaster guitars produced in the 50s feature a heavy milled jack cup, with a sharp inner edge, whilst post-52 guitars have a receptacle made of pressed steel. The latter variant survived through the decades but it has been discarded on more recent production models.

• STRING FERRULES

The Telecaster guitars produced between 1950 and 1966 have recessed string ferrules which are flush with the body. On post-1966 models, the ferrules are clearly protruding on the back of the body, but after the CBS spin-off the newly-independant Fender company reverted to flush ferrules.

• MOUNTING SCREWS

A few words about mounting screws and the transition from single slot screws to Phillips heads. All the 1950 models feature slot heads, including the adjustable truss rod bolt. Beginning in 1951 a gradual transition towards Phillips heads was initiated, but Leo Fender was not a man to waste anything and the complete transition stretched over some two years!

In the course of 1951, the truss-rod bolt as well as the screws fastening the neck, the controls plate and the strap buttons changed to Phillips heads. The 4 screws holding the bridge base plate soon followed suit in early 1952 and pickguard screws in late 1952. In Summer 1953 the bridge pickup and the selector switch could still be found mounted with slot head screws, but the transition was eventually completed by the end of 1953.

HOW TO DATE
A TELECASTER

Assessing the age of a Telecaster guitar may be relatively easy on the whole, provided it has not been tampered with or altered. It can be successfully achieved by combining the following elements:

- the actual markings found on the neck, the body or the pickups at certain periods of time;

- the structural features and discriminating appointments of the various models described in this book;

- the serial number which may help narrow down the period of issue despite the lack of sheer chronology in the Fender serialization schemes.

Should there be any doubt regarding the integrity of an instrument under investigation, it is advisable to compare it side-by-side with a model of similar vintage. Any first-hand experience in Fender manufacturing idiosyncrasies over the years is obviously most useful to ensure that the above elements are definitely original.

DATE MARKINGS

A Fender guitar is best thought of as an "assembled kit," built with components which can be easily taken apart for servicing purposes. The down-side of this typical feature is that it may allow a number of modifications likely to impact upon the integrity of a model. But the up-side is that it provides access to critical information for dating a model! Shortly after production of the Broadcaster began in Fall 1950, it became customary for wood parts – like the neck and the body – to be dated by the employees who had shaped them. Although such markings do precede the actual completion of an instrument by a few weeks or months they are, whenever available (and original!), the safest criterion to assess the age of a Fender guitar.

NECK DATES

The date (if any) is mentioned on the heel of the neck and may be revealed by loosening up the screws securing the neck to the body. Of course, this is not possible on a model like the "Set Neck" Telecaster, which is fitted with a glued-on neck. Since 1950, most Telecaster guitars have been quite consistently dated at the factory, bar a couple of exceptions such as:

- the very first models released prior to Fall 1950;

- the models produced between Spring 1959 and early 1960;

- the models produced between Spring 1973 and late 1981.

Otherwise, different types of date markings have been used at the factory according to the period of production.

- On the necks made between late 1950 and late 1953, the date is pencilled and usually shows the month/day/year in numerals.

For example: "2/1/51" = February 1, 1951

   "8-23-53" = August 23, 1953

- On the necks made between late 1953 and March 1962, the date is still pencilled and indicated in numerals, but the day is no longer systematically mentioned although it can be found on some 1954 necks.

For example: "10-58" = October 1958

   "3-61" = March 1961

These numerals are generally pencilled in black, but they may also be found in red (1953/54) or even in green (rare, in 1950). Besides, they are usually separated by either a slash or a hyphen and up to the mid-50s, the craftsman who shaped the neck frequently added his initials ahead of the date.

For example: "DZ 11/1/50" or "TG 3-54"

There has been some speculation as to the names behind these initials. The most commonly found are "TG," construed to stand for Tadeo Gomez whilst "DZ," featured mostly in 1950, would stand for Dickie Zamora. Other initials such as "AG," "XA" or "TD" also exist, but the names behind them so far remain shrouded in mystery.

As indicated previously, early models like the 1950 Esquires without a truss-rod or the very first Broadcasters are deprived of any neck marking. This has sometimes brought about apocryphal late-40s neck dates, possibly pencilled by proud owners keen to match the official concept that the Broadcaster was introduced in 1948! After Spring 1959, the neck dating procedure was suspended for a few months and resumed in early 1960. During this period, the latest models with a Maple Neck as well as the earliest ones with a rosewood fretboard do not feature any neck date, although they usually carry a body date(!).

- On the necks made between March 1962 and March 1973, the date is no longer pencilled but rubber-stamped in black. This new type of marking reflected an increased sophistication at FENDER in the early 60s, for it not only shows the first three letters of the month and the last two digits of the year, but also the neck width and a specific code for each model in the range.

For example a "3JUN63B" marking belongs to:

- a Telecaster/Esquire neck ("3")

- made in June 1963 ("JUN63")

- with a standard nut width ("B")

It does not refer to a second choice neck made on June 3, 1963!

Unlike the Stratocaster, Telecaster and Esquire necks always kept the same inventory code, i.e. "3", between 1962 and 1973 [see GUITAR IDENTIFICATION by same author for other Fender neck codes]. The letter suffix in the rubber-stamped marking indicates the width at the nut, as per the following code applied to both guitars and basses:

- A means 1 1/2" (=1.500") i.e. narrow

- B means 1 5/8" (=1.625") i.e. standard

- C means 1 3/4" (=1.750") i.e. wide

- D means 1 7/8" (=1.875") i.e. extra wide

Historically, "B" has always been the standard width on Fender guitars, but in the 60s the other sizes were made optional at an extra cost. They are nevertheless quite unusual, especially on Telecaster guitars for which optional neck widths were not listed.

Between 1962 and early 1973 most necks were quite consistently dated at the factory in this way. Omissions are possible, albeit fairly scarce. Left-handed necks may come without any marking and Rosewood Telecasters, too, are often deprived of any neck date although they sometimes feature a barely visible black ink stamp. Otherwise, a number of necks made in the late 60s feature a distinct type of marking, usually in green with either smaller or taller digits.

For example: "3 247 9 9B" on Telecaster Custom #255985

Based upon the specific appointments of the guitars fitted with such markings, this appears to have been essentially used in 1969. At that time, CBS/FENDER may have intended to modify its inventory neck codes for internal purposes, but the plan fell through... temporarily!

- The necks made after early 1973 feature an entirely new type of marking, which unfortunately does not suggest any obvious production date. The stamped code is more elaborate but to the detriment of any instant dating.

For example "1303 3341" on Telecaster #605659

The first group of 4 digits is meant to indicate the model and the type of fretboard, i.e. "13"= Telecaster and "03"= Maple Neck. Based on the reference numbers then used by FENDER for the Telecaster range, the other codes are "07" for the Custom, "08" for the Deluxe and "30" for the Thinline, whilst a rosewood fretboard neck carries a "01" suffix. Unfortunately, the last 4 digits are less decipherable and their actual meaning is not known to this author! These 8-digit markings (sometimes 7-digit only) may be stamped in black, red or green. For some reason, however, the Deluxe does not follow this reasoning and its neck usually comes with a specific "TEL-DELX.73" marking.

THE *Fender* TELECASTER

Over the years, Fender used different types of neck markings. From top to bottom: 1951, 1953, 1958, 1965, 1969, 1974 and 1988.

Early 50s body date pencilled in the neck pocket.

Early 50s date marking written on a piece of masking tape in the control cavity.

Late 60s pickup date pencilled on the bottom plate.

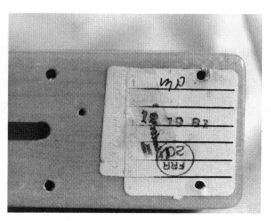

Fully dated inspection tag on a 1981 neck beel.

Late 50s body date pencilled in the bridge pickup cavity.

Mid-70s date marking (1974) ink-stamped on the underplate of a 70s humbucker.

The "137825" marking on this pot indicates that it was made by CTS during the 25th week of 1958.

- After CBS called in a new management team in 1981, the inventory code system was dropped and clear date markings were resumed, albeit in different manners over the years. At first, numerals (MM DD YY) were rubber-stamped for a short time on standard models, but FENDER soon changed for smaller and more explicit date markings in 1983.

For example: "OCT 12 1983" on Elite #E316667

Vintage Telecaster necks, however, were produced from the outset with an old-style marking pencilled à la 1952, i.e. MM-DD-YY.

For example: "10-14-83" on Vintage reissue #4720

When the production of guitars resumed at the Corona plant in late 1985, the same dating procedures were reinstated, but old-style pencilled markings may now also be found on non-vintage models.

For example: "11 10 88" on American Std #E806098

Rubber-stamped markings have not been discontinued though and on the threshold of the 90s, they are still applied with either black or red ink.

BODY DATES

The body date on a Telecaster guitar may be found (if any) either in the neck pocket or in the lead pickup routing. However, it should be mentioned right away that over the years body dates have not been applied quite as consistently as neck dates. In fact, experience shows that body markings are common between late 1950 and 1963 only. Besides, they are mostly visible on guitars with a light finish such as Blonde or sunburst, but they typically do not show under an opaque custom colour finish.

- On the bodies made between 1950 and late 1953, the date is usually pencilled in the neck pocket according to the month/day/year of production. Like contemporary neck markings, it goes with the initials or the first name of the employee who did the job.

For example: "TG 8/13/51" on No-Caster #1126

"Eddie 8/6/52" on Telecaster #3180

Other signatures likely to be found during this period are "EM" (same as Eddie and purportedly meant to indicate an employee by the name of Eddie Mendoza), "TAD" (for Tadeo?), "Kenny," "IP" or "JS."

- On the bodies made after late 1953, the actual day of production as well as the initials of the employee were gradually phased out. Between 1954 and 1963, the date simply consists of a fraction showing the month and the year.

For example: "5-55" on Esquire #7886

"12-60" on Telecaster Custom #54746

Up to 1955 the date is pencilled in the neck pocket, but by 1956 it is relocated in the lead pickup routing, right under the bridge plate. Dates may still appear on some 1964 guitars, but the whole process was basically discontinued in late 1963

More often than not, neck and body dates do not coincide on one guitar. In the early days, production was obviously not that abundant by modern standards and both neck and body were frequently made during the same month (but usually not on the same day!). On a 1952 guitar, though, it is quite common to find dates which are one month apart. With a gradual increase in production during the 1950s, the gap between both dates may usually reach anything like one to three months. The following sample of referenced Telecasters and Esquires further illustrate this point:

MODEL	S/N	NECK DATE	BODY DATE
Broadcaster	0017	11/1/50	11/7/50
Telecaster	1201	10/20/51	10/18/51
Esquire	3566	7/2/52	6/12/52
Telecaster	4198	3/54	2/54
Esquire	7886	4/55	5/55
Esquire	33783	11/58	1/59
Tele.Custom	54746	9/60	12/60

Some guitars may sometimes feature a much bigger gap between neck and body dates. If both parts are originally matched, it simply reflects a left-over neck or body unduly put in storage before hitting the finishing line. Having said that, it may also indicate that either one of the two has been swapped at some point in time, not necessarily at the Fender factory!

Finally, it should be noted that body dates were still applied in 1959/60, when the dating of necks was temporarily suspended, and they are very useful to assess the age of guitars made during this period.

For example: Telecaster Custom #38820 with no neck date but "5-59" pencilled in the lead pickup routing

After 1963, the body dating procedure was never resumed as such but dates may surface on 70s and 80s guitars, either pencilled or stamped among names and various markings in the neck pocket.

For example: "11 20 80" on Telecaster #S838365

These markings are rather inspection dates generated by the control checks enforced by CBS in an attempt to remedy a deteriorating quality in production. Whenever available, they may be useful to date instruments otherwise deprived of neck dates.

Owing to its greater availability over the years, the neck date is generally accepted as the prime reference to log the "birthday" of a Fender guitar. This being said, it does precede the actual date of completion and sale of the instrument by at least a few weeks and often a few months.

OTHER MARKINGS

Besides neck and body, a Telecaster guitar may feature other markings likely to assist with its dating over certain periods of time. Two categories of markings are more particularly interesting in this respect:

- The early models produced between 1951 and 1955 usually have a date pencilled on a piece of masking tape, located in the control cavity. This piece of tape is affixed either on the side or on the bottom of the cavity routing and in 1953/55 it also indicates a female first name.

For example: "8-10-51" on No-Caster #1043

"Mary 5-12-53" on Telecaster #2323

These markings basically indicate the very day the pickups and wiring harness were installed into the body and at times the name of the woman who did it (usually Mary, Gloria, Virginia or Carolyn). Until 1955 Telecaster guitars thus have up to THREE dates to refer to, as illustrated in the following table:

MODEL	S/N	NECK DATE	BODY DATE	CONTROLS TAPE
No-Caster	1924	TD 8/8/51	JS 8/14/51	8/20/51
Telecaster	3849	8-23-53	Tad 7-7-53	Gloria 8/26/53
Telecaster	8503	7-55	7-55	Mary 8-10-55

After 1955, the piece of masking tape ceased to be affixed probably because of a more substantial workload at the factory. Too bad, it is most handy to quickly assess the age of an old Telly without having to unscrew the neck.

- In 1964 FENDER began to mention a date on the bottom plate of most of its pickups bobbins. On Telecaster guitars it usually does not show on the neck pickup because of a too narrow bottom with protruding magnets. Only the bridge pickup is likely to feature any date, but it is not always easy to actually see it because of the shielding copper plate.

During the 60s and 70s, three different types of markings were thus successively applied:

- on the pickups with a black fibre bottom plate, the date is rubber-stamped in clear with yellow ink (e.g. "FEB 10 64")

- on the light grey bottom plates first used in 1965, the date is hand-written in clear with black ink (e.g. "9-6-66")

- on the dark grey bottom plate introduced in about 1969, FENDER switched over to a 3 to 6-digit code, rubber-stamped in black or red, which may be deciphered to indicate the year.

For example: Thinline #231917 (neck date "JAN69") with "52 9" on pickup (9=1969)

Telecaster #395620 (neck date "OCT72") with "479 73" on pickup (73=1973)

- on the 70s humbucking pickups a similar code is rubber-stamped in black or yellow on the metal bottom plate.

For example: Thinline #525896 (no neck date) with "24 44 74" on pickups (74=1974)

Although some of these code numbers may sometimes look like actual dates, too many exceptions do not fit the scheme. Suffice it to say that the final digit(s) usually show the year, which is of help on the 70s guitars without any neck date. It should be borne in mind, however, that the code (if any) was stamped when the pickup was finished and stored, hence a possible gap of a couple of weeks if not months prior to finding its way on a guitar.

- Finally, mention should be made of the potentiometers code which, although less reliable to date a guitar, may be useful to cross-check the integrity of its wiring harness. All US made potentiometers are stamped with a 6 to 7-digit code reading "XXX(Y)YWW", in which:

- XXX is the manufacturer's code (e.g. 137=CTS; 304=Stackpole.)

- YY shows the year (1 digit in the 50s, 2 digits thereafter)

- WW shows the week in the year

For example:

"304021" is on a Stackhole pot from the 21st week of 1950

"1376036" is on a CTS pot from the 36th week of 1960

"3047305" is on a Stackhole pot from the 5th week of 1973

"1378821" is on a CTS pot from the 21st week of 1988

This code is not to be confused with the part reference numbers frequently stamped on the pot by the manufacturer for inventory purposes. For instance, the full markings on the pots of a 1969 Esquire read as follows "032367 250K A 1376642" in which:

- "032367" is the part number for a 250K audio pot

- "1376642" is the dating code (CTS 42nd week of 1966)

Overall, the pot code may be of assistance to crosscheck the year of issue of models deprived of any neck and/or body date. But it should be borne in mind that pots are high volume items likely to be ordered in thousands and stored for some time. In the early 70s, many Fenders were still fitted with pots dating from 1966, ordered in vast quantities by CBS shortly after the take-over!

For example: Rosewood Telecaster #330774 (neck date "SEP71") with pots coded "1376636" i.e. 36th week of 1966

SERIAL NUMBERS

Despite a lack of perfect chronology in the Fender serialization schemes, it is nevertheless possible to derive some useful information from them. No real precise dating can be achieved from a serial number alone, but it may help narrow down a period of issue within a 1 to 3 year band. The following schemes have been successively used by FENDER on Telecaster guitars since 1950.

THE ORIGINAL SERIES: 1950 - 1963

When the first electric Spanish guitar was introduced in 1950, it came with a 4-digit serial number stamped on the bridge plate which, despite its format, did not dovetail into the schemes already in use on other products such as lap steel guitars. It can be therefore assumed that the serialization of the all-new model theoretically started with #0001 (NB a zero counts as one digit) and progressed on a roughly cumulative basis.

Although correct in principle, this theory is not entirely corroborated by the actual numbers found on 1950 guitars. For instance, the numbers of some of the very few documented Esquires without a truss-rod read #0013, #0043 or #0087 and are indeed higher than those of some later guitars with a truss-rod. In fact, the numbers on the Spanish guitars made in 1950 do vary substantially and may show jumps in tens, hundreds and even thousands, whilst production did not probably exceed a hundred guitars or so. Such an erratic pattern is largely verified during the early 50s with serial numbers stamped on the bridge plate. Thus, a '52 model may be fitted with a number in the 3000s whilst one from '53 or '54 may show a lower number in the 2000s.

For example: Esquire #2782 with a 4-54 neck date

Telecaster #2961 with a 12-53 neck date

Telecaster #3686 with a 12-52 neck date

Esquire #3735 with a 7-52 neck date

This leads to the conclusion that during the early 50s:

- serial numbers were not used sequentially on a cumulative basis, i.e. the lower the number, the older the instrument

- there is no strict correlation between neck dates and serial numbers, which were basically allotted at random regardless of the period of issue

- serial numbers were not stamped on an "ad hoc" basis, but probably pre-stamped in quantities.

- From 1950 up to 1954 numbers were stamped on the bridge plate, below the words "FENDER PAT.PEND.," between the lead pick-up and the saddles. Upon closer examination, one could observe that the last numeral is often slightly off-line with the preceding three (like on the earliest Stratocaster numbers stamped on the vibrato back plate). This has sometimes fueled speculation that numbers on the earliest Telecaster guitars were originally of a 3-digit format and that a 4th digit was added later(?). In fact, the slightly off 4th digit certainly originated in a two-step process (or a faulty machine) because the whole number is anyway well centered below the words "FENDER PAT. PEND."

- In the course of 1954 FENDER ceased to stamp the number on the bridge plate and relocated it on the upper edge of the neck plate. Simultaneously, the company also put an end to the three parallel, yet identical in format, serialization schemes used so far on the Telecaster & Esquire, the Precision Bass and the Stratocaster. By then, bridge numbers had reached numbers in the 5000s and the higher bridge number known so far to this author is #5368, but it may well not be the highest ever. Based upon sampled neck dates it appears that the transition between bridge numbers and neck plate numbers took place over Summer 1954 without any major overlap.

For example: Telecaster #4044 (B/P) with a 9-54 neck date

Telecaster #4683 (B/P) with a 8-54 neck date

Esquire #7043 (N/P) with a 10-54 neck date

Esquire #7336 (N/P) with a 8-54 neck date

This short table shows once more the lack of strict correlation between serial numbers and production dates. The latest bridge numbers are not necessarily the higher, e.g. in the 5000s. Likewise the earliest neck plate numbers are not systematically in the high 5000s or low 6000s.

- From late 1954 onwards, numbers quickly progressed within a basic 4 and 5-digit format from high 5000s up to 90000s, as they were indiscriminatingly applied to an ever-expanding Fender range. In less than nine years numbers in the high 90000s were finally reached in early 1963. Incidentally, this increased production makes it somewhat easier to do groupings with numbers and derive some information from them for dating purposes. For instance, most numbers in the 40000s are found on guitars made between late 1959 and mid-1960.

As production grew in Fullerton, larger quantities of neck plates were stamped, but a few batches came up with peculiar features during the mid-to-late 1950s. For instance:

- between 1955 and 1956, some plates were stamped with 5-digit numbers beginning with "0" instead of straight 4-digit numbers.

For example: Telecaster #06998 with a 1-55 neck date

Esquire #08970 with a 5-56 neck date

- between 1957 and early 1958, some numbers were stamped with a preceding dash or hyphen, making them look like "minus" numbers.

For example: Esquire #–19547 with a 6-57 neck date

Esquire #–20020 with a 2-57 neck date

- between late 1957 and mid-1958, some plates were stamped with 6-digit numbers beginning with "0" instead of straight 5-digit numbers.

For example: Telecaster #023312 with a 10-57 neck date

Telecaster #028343 with a 4-58 neck date

- between late 1957 and late 1958, some plates were double stamped and feature two different numbers on each side. As a rule, the visible number is of the 6-digit type beginning with a zero whilst the concealed number stamped on the underside is of the minus type.

  For example: Telecaster #024154 & – 24785 with a 12-57 neck date

- between late 1959 and mid-1960, some numbers were stamped on the lower edge of the neck plate instead of the upper edge.

Despite these peculiar features, all the numbers used between 1954 and 1963 belong to the same basic serialization scheme.

THE "L" SERIES: 1963 - 1965

The "L" series, as it is currently nicknamed, is also in all probability the result of a stamping mistake, even though the "Leo's theory" is tempting. When numbers in the 90000s hit the assembly line, fresh neck plates were stamped but, for some reason, they did not turn out with numbers in the 100000s but with numbers reading L00001s. In other words, their first digit is not "1" but "L", hence the "L series" designation.

The earliest L-numbers – but not necessarily the lowest – appeared on guitars made in late 1962 and they overlapped with the latest numbers from the original series. The bulk of the L-series is, however, primarily found on instruments made between early 1963 and mid-1965. A few L-numbers may surface on later instruments with for instance an early 1966 neck date, but these are rather exceptions. Otherwise, the L-series does not represent a major evolution and it ran from L00001 up to L99999 on a roughly cumulative basis, albeit without any strict sequential order. Production-wise, it is worth noting that it was used up in less than three years, which allows for some groupings because of a tighter distribution over a limited period of time. By and large, instruments with L-numbers are often considered today as the last specimens from the Leo Fender era.

THE "F" SERIES: 1965 - 1976

When L-numbers in the 90000s came in sight by Spring 1965, CBS/FENDER logically moved up to 6-digit numbers in the 100000s but without a "L" prefix. The newer plates came up, however, with the typical Fender backward "F" conspicuously stamped below the number,hence the "F-series" nickname.

The earliest F-numbers appeared in mid-1965, but until the end of the year they overlapped with the latest L-numbers.Because of a drastically increased production after the mid-60s, F-numbers rapidly moved in thousands and ran from 100000s up to 700000s in about 11 years. Again, no specific sequential order was put to effect and, due to the dissemination of numbers over a wide range of products, groupings are only approximate to within 2 to 4 years!

For example: Telecaster #300612 with a MAR70 neck date

Telecaster #309661 with a JUL71 neck date

Telecaster #310967 with a APR72 neck date

Telecaster #316987 with a JAN73 neck date

For the guitars produced until early 1973 (i.e. with numbers up to the low 400000s), it is possible to work out a very primitive dating chart thanks to the available neck dates. The guitars released thereafter (i.e. with numbers from 400000s up to 700000s) are more of a problem, but the following broad guidelines, relating to actual shipping dates, were supplied by CBS/FENDER a few years ago:

- 400000s numbers: April 1973 up to September 1976
- 500000s numbers: September 1973 up to September 1976
- 600000s numbers: August 1974 up to August 1976
- 700000s numbers: September 1976 up to December 1976

HEADSTOCK NUMBERS: 1976 - PRESENT

In late 1976, FENDER ceased to stamp the serial number on the neck plate and began to incorporate it into the headstock decal. Almost simultaneously, a new serialization scheme meant to indicate the year of issue was devised to replace the roughly cumulative formula in use since 1950. New style 7-digit numbers were then introduced, with a basic 2-digit prefix for the year of issue plus 5 digits for the identification of the guitar.

The first prefix briefly used was "76" and the numbers read 76xxxxx, with "76" in bolder numerals than the x's.

Within a couple of weeks, though, the "76" prefix was deleted and replaced by "S6". This change definitely implemented the system still in use today, whereby the first letter shows the decade (S=seventies) and the following numeral the year in the decade (6=1976, 7=1977, etc...). The 1980s logically brought in a new prefix letter (E=eighties) and in the course of 1990 FENDER began to order new decals prefixed with "N" for nineties.

This scheme looks perfectly alright in principle, but unfortunately it is not that reliable to date the guitars made by FENDER in the USA. Here are the reasons why.

- At the end of each year, new decals reflecting the change in prefix were ordered in thousands from a subcontracting company (MEYERCORD up to the early 80s and ASSOCIATED SILK SCREEN PRINTING since then). Problem is that the old decals were not instantly discarded at the turn of the year, particularly if there were plenty of unused left-overs. Therefore, the previous year's decals often continued to be used into the new year, despite having a no-longer-correct prefix. For instance, many guitars actually made in 1980 and 1981 were released with "S9" numbers.

- After CBS decided to sell FENDER in mid-1984, no "E5" decals were ordered and until the closedown of the Fullerton plant in early 1985, guitars were shipped with "E4" and even "E3" decals. When the newly-independant FENDER company resumed its manufacturing activities in the USA at the end of 1985, it had a sizeable quantity of "E4" decals to use up. Bearing in mind the initially limited output of the new Corona plant and the few models such decals were applied to, it took until 1988 to dry up the left-over E4 decals. In other words, E5, E6 and E7 decals were never applied to US made instruments, even though they do exist on Japanese made guitars! Besides, some guitars meant for export to Europe or Japan were also briefly serialized with an "EE" prefix" instead of "E4".

- In 1990, FENDER was still primarily using E9 decals, but around Summer it was finally decided to order nineties decals. The trouble is that they did not turn up with a "N0" but with a "N9" prefix (=1999!), thanks to what appears to be a blunder from the subcontracting company. Business obviously means that those N9 decals have not been thrown away and they are currently applied to both 1990 and 1991 instruments.

Consequently, notwithstanding their apparently impeccable logic, 7-digit numbers meant for standard models are not that reliable for dating purposes. The following guidelines kindly supplied by FENDER clearly evidence numerous overlaps and hiccups.

- S7 + 5 digits: January 1977 up to April 1978
- S8 + 5 digits: December 1977 up to December 1978
- S9 + 5 digits: November 1978 up to August 1981
- EO + 5 digits: June 1979 up to January 1981
- E1 + 5 digits: December 1980 up to January 1982
- E2 + 5 digits: December 1981 up to January 1983
- E3 + 5 digits: December 1982 up to January 1985
- E4 + 5 digits: December 1983 up to January 1985
- E8 + 5 digits: April 1988 up to January 1989
- E9 + 5 digits: December 1989 up to September 1990

Over the 1976-1990 period, the above 7-digit numbers are found on the following production Telecasters: Standard, Thinline, Custom, Deluxe, Elite, American Standard, James Burton and Tele Plus.

OTHER NUMBERS: 1976 - PRESENT

However, not all Telecaster guitars made since 1976 have been fitted with the above serialization scheme. Beginning in 1981, several models were released with specific numbers.

- THE COLLECTOR'S SERIES

  The Black & Gold Telecaster produced between mid-1981 and mid-1983 is characterized by a 7-digit headstock number prefixed with "CE."

1980s Vintage Reissue number. Note the dot stamped below the numerals to avoid any possible confusion with original 1950s bridge plates.

rly 50s serial number stamped on the bridge plate.

Mid-50s number stamped on the neck plate.

L-series serial number.

F-series serial number.

Mid-70s number stamped on a Thinline with Tilt Neck.

"E3" number (=1983)

1990 numbers should have been prefixed with "N0" but due to a mistake in procurement the first batch delivered to the factory read "N9" (=1999!).

"E9" number (=1989)

en digit headstock numbers were allegedly ised to indicate the year of production (e.g. 5358=1978), but they are not always a reliable rce of information. For instance, the body of ecaster #S838365 features an inspection tag ed November 1980.

Custom Shop 4-digit number applied to the back of the headstock. Also note Custom Shop label featuring the name of the luthier responsible for the instrument.

BRIDGE PLATE NUMBERS/NECK DATES: 1950-1954

S/N	DATE	MODEL	S/N	DATE	MODEL	S/N	DATE	MODEL	S/N	DATE	MODEL	S/N	DATE	MODEL
0017	11-50	Broadcaster	0724	2-51	Broadcaster	1699	8-51	No-Caster	2961	12-53	Telecaster	4060	10-52	Telecaster
0052	12-50	Broadcaster	0742	12-50	Broadcaster	1769	12-51	Telecaster	3020	12-53	Telecaster	4123	11-53	Telecaster
0070	10-50	Broadcaster	0748	9-51	Telecaster	1788	3-52	Esquire	3065	7-52	Telecaster	4124	2-53	Esquire
0089	11-50	Broadcaster	0856	5-51	Esquire	1895	9-51	Telecaster	3180	7-52	Telecaster	4198	3-54	Telecaster
0115	10-50	Broadcaster	0984	8-51	Telecaster	1899	11-50	Broadcaster	3224	5-52	Telecaster	4303	3-52	Telecaster
0149	11-50	Broadcaster	0997	10-51	Telecaster	1924	8-51	No-Caster	3247	1-54	Telecaster	4520	7-52	Telecaster
0210	7-51	Esquire	1043	8-51	No-Caster	2023	10-53	Esquire	3342	9-52	Telecaster	4551	4-53	Esquire
0213	12-50	Broadcaster	1072	9-51	Telecaster	2112	8-52	Telecaster	3377	2-53	Telecaster	4585	9-54	Telecaster
0235	11-50	Broadcaster	1120	12-51	Telecaster	2190	7-53	Esquire	3454	11-52	Esquire	4617	4-54	Telecaster
0293	4-52	Telecaster	1126	8-51	No-Caster	2289	12-53	Telecaster	3491	1-54	Telecaster	4651	10-53	Esquire
0298	10-50	Broadcaster	1131	8-51	Telecaster	2302	3-53	Telecaster	3566	7-52	Esquire	4670	8-52	Telecaster
0460	11-50	Broadcaster	1182	1-51	No-Caster	2339	11-52	Telecaster	3606	6-54	Telecaster	4676	8-54	Telecaster
0471	1-51	Esquire	1201	10-51	Telecaster	2374	6-53	Telecaster	3686	12-52	Telecaster	4700	8-53	Telecaster
0582	4-51	No-Caster	1288	12-51	Telecaster	2384	12-53	Telecaster	3735	7-52	Esquire	4782	9-52	Esquire
0599	11-50	Broadcaster	1292	6-51	Esquire	2409	2-53	Telecaster	3776	11-51	Telecaster	4817	7-53	Telecaster
0606	1-51	Esquire	1427	8-51	No-Caster	2547	11-50	Broadcaster	3849	8-53	Telecaster	4902	11-52	Telecaster
0678	11-52	Telecaster	1457	12-51	Telecaster	2580	10-52	Esquire	3928	4-53	Esquire	5031	9-53	Telecaster
0683	11-50	Broadcaster	1569	11-51	Telecaster	2741	4-54	Telecaster	3962	9-53	Esquire	5171	6-53	Telecaster
0690	2-51	Esquire	1587	12-52	Telecaster	2871	7-52	Esquire	3995	6-53	Telecaster	5204	7-52	Esquire
0712	5-51	No-Caster	1688	2-51	Broadcaster	2949	4-54	Esquire	4046	1-53	Telecaster	5279	5-52	Telecaster

NECK PLATE NUMBERS/NECK DATES: 1954-1973

S/N	DATE	MODEL	S/N	DATE	MODEL	S/N	DATE	MODEL	S/N	DATE	MODEL	S/N	DATE	MODEL
5883	5-55	Esquire	35695	4-59	Telecaster	L01127	APR63	Telecaster	103995	JUL65	Telecaster	250748	MAY68	Tele.Custom
6608	3-55	Telecaster	36560	3-59	Telecaster	L01180	FEB63	Telecaster	104906	MAY65	Telecaster	254241	MAY69	Esquire
6711	9-55	Esquire	40644	10-58	Telecaster	L01635	JUN62	Esquire	112172	SEP66	Telecaster	259947	MAY69	Tele.Thinline
06998	1-55	Telecaster	44157	6-60	Tele.Custom	L02950	MAR63	Telecaster	115147	DEC65	Esquire	262281	JUL69	Tele.Custom
7307	4-55	Telecaster	44282	8-60	Tele.Custom	L03475	APR63	Esquire	122654	FEB66	Tele.Custom	271920	JAN68	Telecaster
7336	8-54	Esquire	48919	3-60	Telecaster	L04064	JUN63	Telecaster	125079	DEC65	Telecaster	272501	MAR71	Tele.Thinline
7359	10-54	Telecaster	49518	5-60	Telecaster	L07189	DEC62	Esquire	128331	APR66	Telecaster	275152	SEP69	Telecaster
8019	7-55	Telecaster	50920	5-60	Tele.Custom	L10102	MAY63	Telecaster	132409	MAR66	Telecaster	280816	AUG70	Tele.Thinline
8099	1-55	Telecaster	51032	6-60	Esquire	L10439	MAR63	Telecaster	147824	MAY66	Tele.Custom	286193	JUL68	Tele.Thinline
8503	7-55	Telecaster	54360	8-60	Esq.Custom	L12092	JUN63	Tele.Custom	149257	SEP66	Telecaster	295859	SEP67	Telecaster
08970	5-56	Esquire	54746	9-60	Tele.Custom	L13181	DEC62	Esquire	155431	JUL66	Telecaster	297863	NOV70	Telecaster
09394	12-55	Telecaster	58020	10-60	Tele.Custom	L13281	JUN63	Telecaster	161804	AUG66	Tele.Custom	299736	MAY71	Telecaster
09996	2-56	Esquire	59002	12-60	Esquire	L15953	OCT63	Tele.Custom	167924	OCT66	Telecaster	300612	MAR70	Tele.Thinline
10083	8-55	Telecaster	60138	2-61	Esquire	L16550	OCT63	Esq.Custom	170416	MAR66	Telecaster	303997	JAN71	Telecaster
11257	6-56	Esquire	61810	4-61	Telecaster	L19017	AUG63	Telecaster	172178	AUG66	Esquire	307466	OCT70	Tele.Custom
12594	9-56	Esquire	63204	5-61	Tele.Custom	L19716	JUN63	Telecaster	177112	NOV66	Tele.Custom	310143	JUL71	Tele.Thinline
14350	10-56	Telecaster	66499	7-61	Esquire	L20349	NOV63	Tele.Custom	182112	JAN67	Telecaster	316337	APR71	Telecaster
16035	11-56	Esquire	66670	8-61	Esquire	L21743	NOV63	Tele.Custom	183957	SEP67	Telecaster	324720	OCT71	Telecaster
16361	7-56	Esquire	69035	6-61	Tele.Custom	L23025	OCT62	Telecaster	185952	APR67	Esquire	325015	JUN71	Telecaster
17849	8-57	Esquire	69051	10-61	Telecaster	L24814	OCT63	Esquire	193463	AUG66	Esquire	325034	JAN72	Telecaster
-19054	1-57	Telecaster	70460	10-61	Esquire	L24860	NOV63	Telecaster	195769	OCT67	Telecaster	330507	FEB72	Telecaster
-20077	2-57	Telecaster	71059	12-61	Telecaster	L29360	NOV63	Tele.Custom	198676	JUL67	Tele.Custom	330774	SEP71	Tele.Rosewood
-20460	9-57	Esquire	71471	8-61	Telecaster	L34459	SEP63	Telecaster	201146	JUL67	Telecaster	338182	FEB73	Telecaster
-21616	7-55	Esquire	72527	12-61	Telecaster	L34779	DEC63	Telecaster	205838	NOV67	Tele.Custom	341020	JAN72	Telecaster
023312	10-57	Telecaster	72711	10-61	Telecaster	L35905	APR63	Esq.Custom	208410	SEP67	Esq.Custom	344226	NOV71	Telecaster
023154 } -24785	12-57	Telecaster	76816	3-62	Tele.Custom	L36559	NOV63	Tele.Custom	212517	DEC67	Telecaster	354239	SEP72	Tele.Thinline
			77522	1-62	Tele.Custom	L37511	SEP63	Esquire	213820	JUN68	Telecaster	355205	APR72	Telecaster
024760	2-58	Telecaster	78794	3-62	Tele.Custom	L39957	AUG64	Telecaster	214289	DEC67	Esquire	357231	OCT71	Tele.Thinline
025167	12-57	Esquire	81745	12-61	Esquire	L40771	SEP63	Tele.Custom	217178	FEB68	Tele.Custom	362789	FEB73	Telecaster
026461	6-58	Telecaster	83502	MAR63	Telecaster	L42308	DEC63	Esq.Custom	220792	OCT68	Esquire	367046	AUG72	Tele.Thinline
028343	4-58	Telecaster	85944	3-62	Tele.Custom	L50451	APR64	Tele.Custom	221348	AUG68	Tele.Thinline	371447	JUN72	Telecaster
29643	9-58	Esquire	86255	12-61	Telecaster	L69410	DEC64	Telecaster	223388	SEP67	Telecaster	371900	JAN73	Telecaster
30134	10-58	Esquire	87551	MAY62	Esq.Custom	L72906	JUN65	Telecaster	227021	JAN69	Tele.Paisley	382821	MAR72	Tele.Custom
31418	1-59	Telecaster	91245	8-60	Esquire	L78135	JUL65	Telecaster	230305	JUL69	Esquire	383098	OCT72	Tele.Custom
31619	2-59	Esquire	93398	MAY62	Telecaster	L81798	FEB65	Telecaster	230556	DEC68	Tele.Thinline	393694	NOV72	Telecaster
32577	10-58	Telecaster	93875	JUN62	Esq.Custom	L87427	FEB65	Telecaster	235630	FEB68	Telecaster	396183	JUN71	Tele.Custom
33159	4-59	Esquire	94745	DEC62	Esquire	L87564	JUN65	Telecaster	241160	MAR68	Tele.Custom	396288	AUG72	Telecaster
33783	11-58	Esquire	95618	JUN62	Telecaster	L87740	AUG65	Tele.Custom	244679	MAY69	Telecaster	407156	FEB73	Telecaster
33986	2-59	Telecaster	97339	MAY63	Tele.Custom	L91472	JUL65	Telecaster	248469	AUG68	Tele.Floral	409981	MAR73	Telecaster
34981	4-59	Telecaster	99817	DEC62	Esquire	L94120	JAN66	Esquire	250107	MAR69	Telecaster	412357	APR72	Telecaster

BASIC NUMBERING SCHEMES:
1950-1990

1950
1951
1952 } 4 digits under the 6000s stamped on bridge plate
1953

1954   4 digits under the 6000s stamped on bridge plate
4 digits under the 10000s stamped on neck plate

1955   4 or 5 digits (beginning with 0) under the 10000s
a few 5 digits in the low to mid-10000s

1956   a few 4 or 5 digits (beginning with 0) under the 10000s
5 digits in the low to mid-10000s

1957   5 digits in the mid to high 10000s
5 digits in the low 20000s

1958   5 or 6 digits (beginning with 0) in the 20000s
5 digits in the low 30000s

1959   5 digits in the 30000s
5 digits in the low 40000s

1960   5 digits in the 40000s and 50000s

1961   5 digits in the 50000s and 60000s
5 digits in the low 70000s

1962   5 digits in the 60000s, 70000s and 80000s
5 digits in the low 90000s

1963   5 digits in the 80000s and 90000s
L+5 digits under the 10000s
L+5 digts in the 10000s and 20000s

1964   L+5 digits in the 20000s, 30000s, 40000s and 50000s

1965   L+5 digits in the 50000s, 60000s, 70000s, 80000s and 90000s
6 digits in the low 100000s

1966   6 digits in the 100000s and low 200000s

1967   6 digits in the high 100000s and low 200000s

1968   6 digits in the mid 200000s

1969   6 digits in the mid to high 200000s
a few 6 digits in the low 300000s

1970   6 digits in the high 200000s and low 300000s

1971   6 digits in the low to mid 300000s

1972   6 digits in the 300000s

1973   6 digits in the high 300000s, 400000s and low 500000s

1974   6 digits in the 400000s, 500000s and low 600000s

1975   6 digits in the high 400000s, 500000s and 600000s

1976   6 digits in the high 500000s, 600000s and low 700000s
a few 76 and S6+5 digits applied with a decal on headstock

1977   S7+5 digits, a few S8+5 digits

1978   S8+5 digits, a few S7 and S9+5 digits

1979   S9+5 digits, a few E0+5 digits

1980   S9 and E0+5 digits, a few E1+5 digits

1981   E1+5 digits, a few S9 and E0+5 digits
except Black & Gold Telecaster: CE+5 digits

1982   E2+5 digits, a few E1 and E3+5 digits
except Black & Gold Telecaster: CE+5 digits
Vintage Telecaster: 4 digits stamped on bridge plate

1983   E3+5 digits, a few E2+5 digits
except Black & Gold Telecaster: CE+5 digits
Vintage Telecaster: 4 digits stamped on bridge plate

1984   E4+5 digits, a few E3+5 digits
except Vintage Telecaster: 4 digits stamped on bridge plate

1985   E4+5 digits, a few E3+5 digits
except Vintage Telecaster: 4 digits stamped on bridge plate

1986   Vintage Telecaster: 4 digits stamped on bridge plate

1987   E4+5 digits
except Vintage Telecaster: 4 digits stamped on bridge plate

1988   E4 and E8+5 digits
except Vintage Telecaster: 4 digits stamped on bridge plate
40th Anniversary: 3-digit number of 300

1989   E9+5 digits, a few E8+5 digits
except Vintage Telecaster: 5 digits stamped on bridge plate
40th Anniversary: 3-digit number of 300

1990   E9 and N9+5 digits
except Vintage Telecaster: 5 digits stamped on bridge plate

• THE VINTAGE SERIES

The '52 reissue introduced in mid-1981 has a serial number stamped on the bridge plate in the early 50s style. Both the Fullerton and the early Corona guitars have a 4-digit number, roughly progressing from 0001s up to 9000s, but 5-digit numbers in the 10000s have since appeared in 1988. Unlike the other vintage models, the number is not prefixed with a "V" but, to avoid any confusion with real 50s guitars, a distinctive dot is stamped below the serial number.

• THE SIGNATURE SERIES

The full production Signature models are theoretically fitted with an 8-digit headstock number, meant as an extension of the standard 7-digit scheme previously described. Their serial number is simply prefixed with "S".

Telecaster-wise, only the James Burton is currently a full production Signature instrument, whilst the other models catalogued (Gatton and Collins) are built to order by the Custom Shop. This may create discrepancies in the style and location of their relevant serial numbers. Unlike Stratocaster Signature models, which feature an 8-digit number prefixed with "S," the Burton has been so far produced with a straight 7-digit number without "S." In other words, its headstock decal is identical to the one found on the American Standard or the Tele Plus.

• THE 40TH ANNIVERSARY TELECASTER

The limited edition Telecaster produced between mid-1988 and early 1990 is characterized by a number ranking each guitar in the 300 batch, e.g. "109 of 300". This composite number is applied with a black decal on the back of the headstock.

• THE CUSTOM SHOP MODELS

The true Custom Shop instruments (i.e. the one-off's) crafted by John Page and his selected team of master luthiers carry a specific 4-digit number. It is usually applied with a small decal on the back of the headstock (black numerals), but it may also be stamped as well on the neck plate. Having said that, the very concept of the Custom Shop implies that a customer has the possibility to ask for a special number for his personalized instrument.

Besides, not all the instruments carrying a Custom Shop label on the headstock are one-offs built from scratch. Some may be "customized" production models and thus keep their standard serial number. Some may belong to a limited run of semi-custom instruments, specially ordered by a dealer/distributor. In this case, they may feature a specific run of numbers on the neck plate or on the headstock. As a matter of fact, the Custom Shop has been recycling in this way quite a few old-style decals from the CBS era.

SUMMARY

For a quick reference, the various serialization schemes used by FENDER on Telecaster guitars since 1950 have been recapped year by year in a global chart. The numbers itemized in this chart apply only to instruments made in the USA and do not encompass Japanese or Korean made Fender/Squier guitars. Besides, the rounding exercise implied by a global chart means that this chart may not exactly fit all of the Telecasters and Esquires ever produced, but it should reflect the average year of issue for most of them.

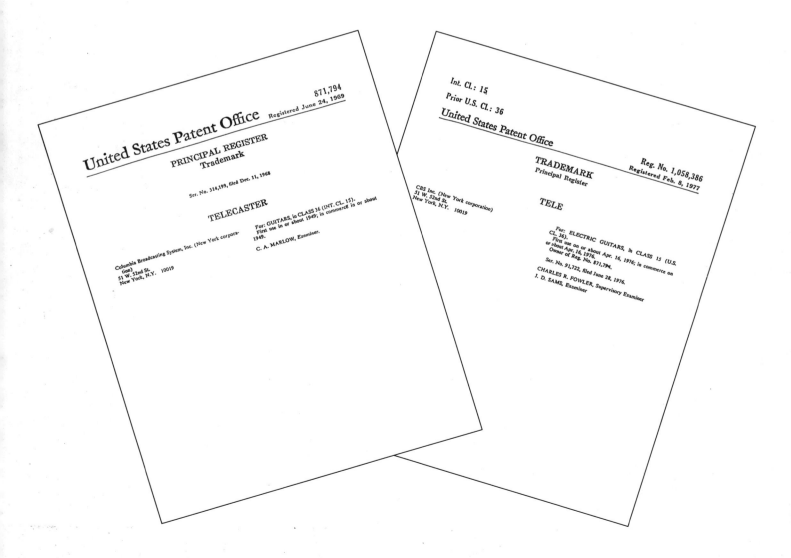